BELIEVING
and EXPERIENCING

A Text for the WJEC GCSE Specification B – Option B

D1741352

by Gavin Craigen and Joy White

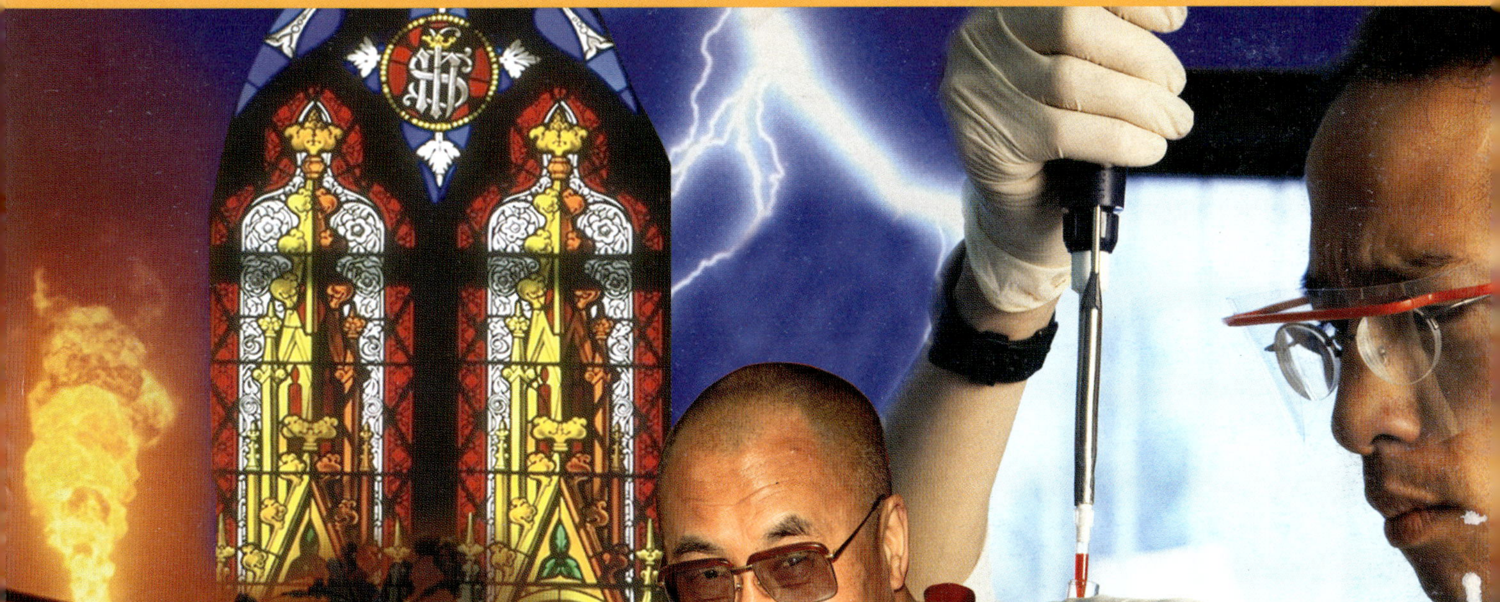

WJEC
CBAC

Hodder & Stoughton

A MEMBER OF THE HODDER HEADLINE GROUP

The publishers would like to thank the following individuals, institutions and companies for permission to reproduce copyright illustrations in this book:

Courtesy Judy Van Hoy: p5; PA Photos/EPA: p10; Corbis/David Pollack: p15 (t); ©Martin Melaugh (http://cain.ulst.ac.uk/melaugh/: p15 (m) and p67 (m,r); AP/Elizabeth Dalziel: p15 (b): Corbis/Flip Schulke: p16 (t): Popperfoto: p16 (b): Corbis/Paul Seheult; Eye Ubiquitous: p17 (t): Corbis/Bettmann: p17 (m): Courtesy Open House: p17 (b): Hulton Getty: p18 (t): Ann & Bury Peerless: p18 (b) and p81 (l); AP/Vadim Ghirda: p22; Christine Osborne Pictures: p56 and p121; James Davis Travel Photography: p57; Eye Ubiquitous/David Cumming: p58; Getty Images/ George Hunter: p59; Alamy.com: p60; Getty Images/Gary Cralle: p61; PA Photos/EPA: p62,66 (t,l), p81 (r), p102 (t,r) and (b,r), p103 (b,r); Corbis/Christine Osborne: p66 (t, r); Rex Features Ltd: p67 (t,l); Courtesy Leicester Council of Faiths: p67 (t,r); Courtesy Christian Publicity Organisation: p67 (b); AP Photos: p66 (m, r); Alamy.com/ Ivan J Belcher: p72; Alamy.com/Christine Osborne: p79 (l) and p83; Corbis/ David Cumming; Eye Ubiquitous: p79 (r); PA Photos/John Stillwell: p88 (b,l and t,r); Alamy.com/ Elvele Images: p88 (t,l); PA Photos: p88 (b,r); AP Photos: p89 (b); Hulton Getty: p91 (l and m); Mary Evans Picture Library: p91 (t,r); Corbis, SABA/Louise Gubb: p91 (b,r); ©1962 & 1981 United Feature Syndicate, Inc. Reproduced with permission: p101 and p107; Corbis/David Turnley: p102 (t,l); Corbis/Peter Turnley: p103 (t) and p103 (b,l); Corbis/Larry Williams: p102 (m); Corbis/Roger Ressmeyer: p102 (b,l); Getty Images/ Bill Ling: p103 (m); Glasgow Museums: The St. Mungo Museum of Religious Life and Art/AKG Images: p111; Corbis/ Angelo Hornak: p114 (t); Corbis/ Arthur Thévenart: p114 (b); TATE, London 2003: p115; Jay Blakesberg/Retna Ltd: p117; Courtesy Salvation Army: p119 (t); CAFOD/Annie Bungeroth: p119 (b,l); Courtesy of CAFOD: p119 (b,r); Courtesy of Karuna Hospice Movement: p120 (l and r); Courtesy of SEWA: p122; Getty Images/Zigy Kaluzny: p123 (l); Courtesy of Jewish Aids Trust: p123 (r); Courtesy Khalsa Aid: p124.

The publishers would also like to thank the following for permission to reproduce material in this book:

"It isn't right to fight" © 1995 John Foster, from *Standing on the Sidelines* (Oxford University Press), included by permission of the author; "A Christian Traffic Warden....accomplishing traffic enforcement" courtesy of The Evening Standard.

Every effort has been made to trace and acknowledge ownership of copyright. The publishers will be glad to make suitable arrangements with any copyright holders whom it has not been possible to contact.

Note about the Internet links in the book. The user should be aware that URLs or web addresses change regularly. Every effort has been made to ensure the accuracy of the URLs provided in this book on going to press. It is inevitable, however, that some will change. It is sometimes possible to find a relocated web page, by just typing in the address of the home page for a website in the URL window of your browser.

All artwork by Daniel Crabbe.

Orders: please contact Bookpoint Ltd, 130 Milton Park, Abingdon, Oxon OX14 4SB. Telephone: (44) 01235 827720. Fax: (44) 01235 400454. Lines are open from 9.00–6.00, Monday to Saturday, with a 24 hour message answering service. You can also order through our website www.hodderheadline.co.uk.

British Library Cataloguing in Publication Data
A catalogue record for this title is available from the British Library

ISBN 0 340 85800 1

First Published 2003
Impression number   10 9 8 7 6 5 4 3 2 1
Year   2009 2008 2007 2006 2005 2004 2003

Copyright © Gavin Craigen, Joy White, 2003

Cover photos: Dalai Lama © Galen Rowell/Corbis; medical technician courtesy of photodisc; all others courtesy of Corel Photo Library.
Typeset by Fakenham Photosetting Ltd, Fakenham, Norfolk
Printed in Italy for Hodder & Stoughton Educational, a division of Hodder Headline Plc, 338 Euston Road, London NW1 3BH

Contents

Levels of Response Grids

Level	AO1 and AO2 Descriptors *(for questions about religious teachings and beliefs)*	4 marks	6 marks
1	A relevant statement of information or explanation which is limited in scope or content. **OR** Makes simple connections between religion and life. Almost no use of specialist language.	1	1
2	An accurate amount of basic information or an appropriate explanation of a central theme or concept. Limited use of specialist language. **OR** Shows informed awareness of the impact of religion on people's lives. Limited use of specialist language.	2	2
3	An account indicating thorough knowledge and understanding of key ideas or concepts. Where appropriate, some use is made of specialist vocabulary. **OR** Shows understanding of the relevance or application of religion. Some use is made of specialist vocabulary.	3	3
	An account indicating thorough knowledge and understanding of key ideas or concepts. Uses and interprets specialist vocabulary in appropriate context. **OR** Shows understanding of the relevance or application of religion. Uses and interprets a range of religious language and terms in appropriate context.	3	4
4	A coherent account showing awareness and insight into religious facts, ideas and explanations. Clear and accurate use of specialist vocabulary. **OR** Demonstrates understanding of different ways in which religion has relevance and application. Clear and accurate use of specialist vocabulary.	4	5
	A coherent account showing awareness and insight into religious facts, ideas and explanations. Specialist vocabulary used extensively and interpreted accurately. **OR** Competently demonstrates understanding of different ways in which religion has relevance and application. Uses specialist vocabulary extensively and interprets them accurately.	4	6

Level	AO3 Descriptor *(for Evaluative Questions – where you use the WAWOS framework)*	Marks
1	A simple appropriate justification of a point of view	1
	And if linked to evidence or suitable example	2
2	An expanded justification of one viewpoint, with appropriate example and/or illustration **OR** A balanced account of alternative viewpoints, with appropriate examples or illustrations	3
	An expanded justification, with examples and/or illustration, using relevant evidence and religious or moral reasoning **OR** A balanced account of alternative viewpoints with appropriate examples and/or illustrations, using relevant evidence and religious or moral reasoning.	4
3	A thorough discussion of the religious and moral aspects of an issue and their implications for the individual and/or for the rest of society, using relevant evidence and religious or moral reasoning **OR** A thorough discussion of the religious and moral aspects of an issue, showing a recognition of some of the complexity of religious issues, using relevant evidence and religious or moral reasoning.	5
	A thorough discussion of the religious and moral aspects of an issue, showing a recognition of some of the complexity of religious issues or their implications for the individual and/or for the rest of society. Makes reasoned judgements based on a range of evidence and well developed arguments	6

1 Religion and Conflict

The Big Picture

What causes conflict between people?

What makes for good relationships between people?

Is it ever right to fight?

How is war avoided?

Questions to ask

Words to know, understand and use: ▼	
CONSCIENCE	
JUST WAR	JUST WAR
PACIFISM	BANNED!
	NON-VIOLENT PROTEST
RECONCILIATION	

Religious teachings to explore:

- Harmony and Tolerance
- War and Violence
- Peace and Reconciliation

What makes for good relationships between people?

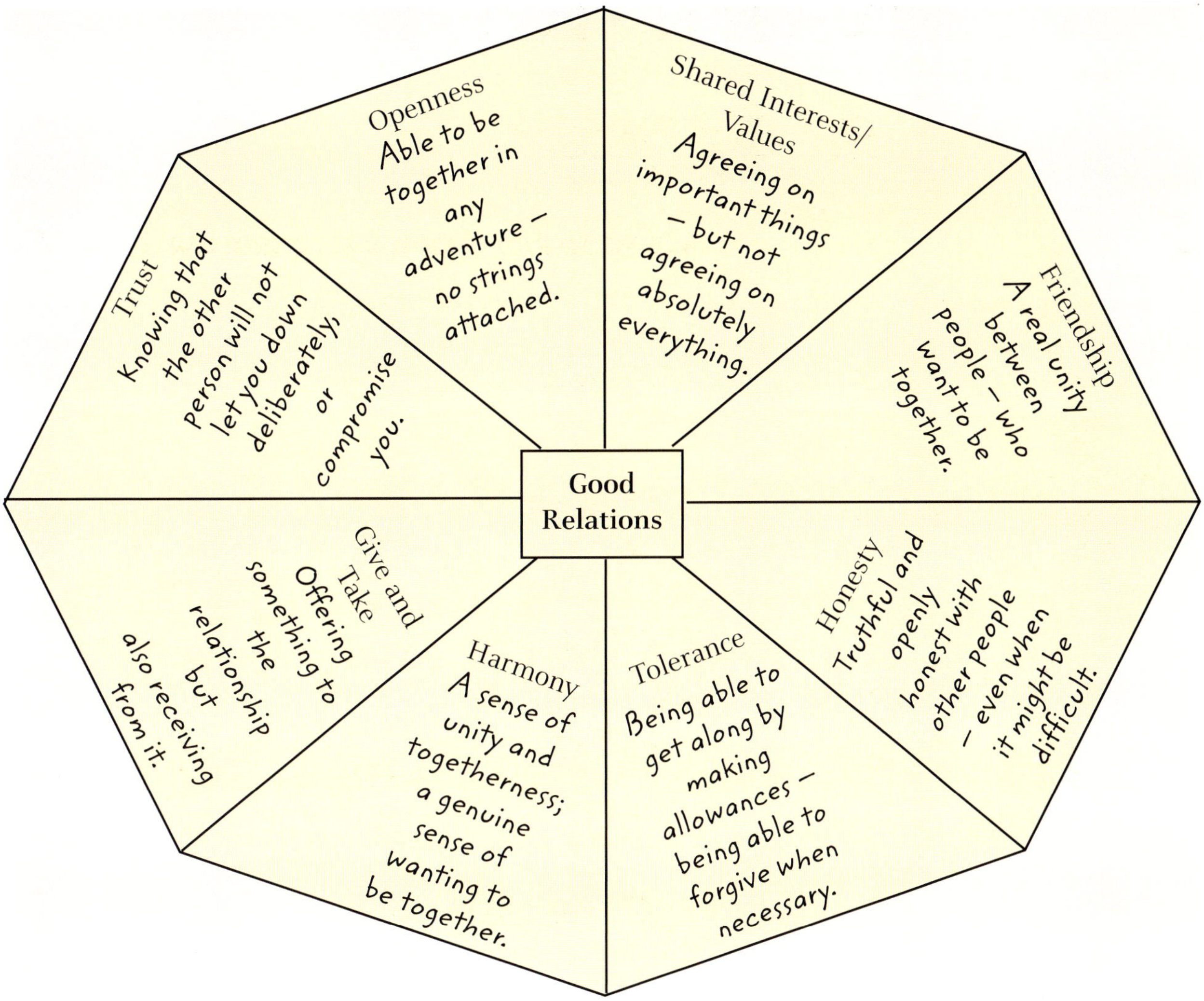

Shared Interests/ Values
Agreeing on important things – but not agreeing on absolutely everything.

Openness
Able to be together in any adventure – no strings attached.

Trust
Knowing that the other person will not let you down deliberately; or compromise you.

Friendship
A real unity between people – who want to be together.

Good Relations

Give and Take
Offering something to the relationship but also receiving from it.

Harmony
A sense of unity and togetherness; a genuine sense of wanting to be together.

Tolerance
Being able to get along by making allowances – being able to forgive when necessary.

Honesty
Truthful and openly honest with other people – even when it might be difficult.

People have found that where these feelings (or at least some of them) are common, then relationships and friendships tend to be strong and longer lasting. Without them, the friendship and togetherness can become strained, and may eventually break down.

Task

- Think about some of your friendships. Which of the above would you say are particularly strong for you and your friends.

- Think about the opposites of the above attitudes – why do you think they lead to difficulties in a relationship?

Disagreement and dispute
What causes conflict between people?

In any friendship or relationship between people, whether just two people or a wider group of friends, there are many different interests and preferences to be considered. It is very easy for someone to feel left out, or feel that their wishes and ideas are not considered. This means that keeping a relationship good and strong needs working at; it needs giving and taking by all the people involved.

Not just differences of opinion, but major arguments that cannot be resolved.

Disagreements

DAILY NEWS

Twin brothers who have not spoken to each other for thirty years.

When people face serious or chronic illness; or perhaps an upheaval like unemployment.

Crises (illness, etc.)

DAILY NEWS

2,000 Jobs to Go

When one person feels they are not being taken account of, or are being used in some way.

Tensions in Relationships

Selfishness

DAILY NEWS

Gardens next to School become litter-dumps.

Physical harm

DAILY NEWS

Revenge Attack in Pub

When someone is harmed physically – other than by accident – they tend to move away.

Betrayal

Being betrayed, unless there is very good reason, is likely to lead to conflict.

Can you think of others?

Dealing with such tensions and situations is not easy, but most religions have some guidelines for relationships with other people. Very often a positive move towards harmony and tolerance is seen as the best way, rather than a direct retaliation or 'sticking up' for ourselves.

In the same manner, most religions expect that where disagreements and disputes happen, they should be sorted out in a friendly open way with people's needs being considered, as well as the good of society or the community as a whole.

Religious teachings about harmony and tolerance.

As the Golden Rule shows, many religions have teachings about the way people should live their lives as believers, and the way they should act and behave towards others.

The Golden Rule *A World-wide Teaching*		
✝	**Christianity**	Do to others what you would have them do to you, for this sums up the Law and the Prophets.
☸	**Buddhism**	Hurt not others in ways that you yourself would find hurtful.
ॐ	**Hinduism**	This is the sum of all righteousness: do nothing to your neighbour which you would not have him do to you.
☪	**Islam**	No one of you is a believer until he desires for his brother that which he desires for himself.
🕎	**Judaism**	What is hateful to you, do not do to your fellow men. That is the entire Law; the rest is commentary.
☬	**Sikhism**	As you deem yourself, so deem others. Then you shall become a partner in heaven.

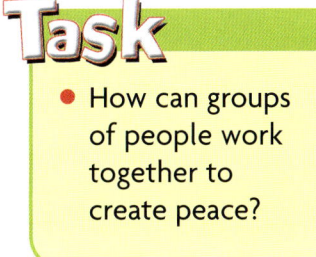

Task

- How can groups of people work together to create peace?

Exam Tip

Quoting the Texts

ALWAYS *use* quotations from sacred texts to support or illustrate your answer;

NEVER just quote or copy texts as an answer.

Q *Jesus said, 'Love your enemies' (Matthew 5:44). How could Christians show love to their enemies? [4]*

Look at the two answers below, and decide what marks you would give to Answer A and Answer B, and why.

Answer A	Answer B
Christians should show love to their enemies because Jesus said love your enemies and pray for those who persecute you.	Christians could show love to their enemies by praying for them even though they are enemies. They could also try and do good to them. Jesus also taught that people should always be willing to forgive others, and not seek revenge.

Conflict, violence and war

Is it ever right to fight?

It isn't right to fight

You said, 'It isn't right to fight,'
But when we watched the news tonight
You shook your fist and said
You wished the tyrant and his cronies dead.
When I asked why,
If it's not right to fight,
You gave a sigh.
You shook your head
And sadly said,
'Sometimes a cause is just,
And, if there is no other way,
Perhaps, you must.'

(J Foster
Standing in the sidelines)

In answering the question, 'Is it ever right to fight', many religious believers give two answers.

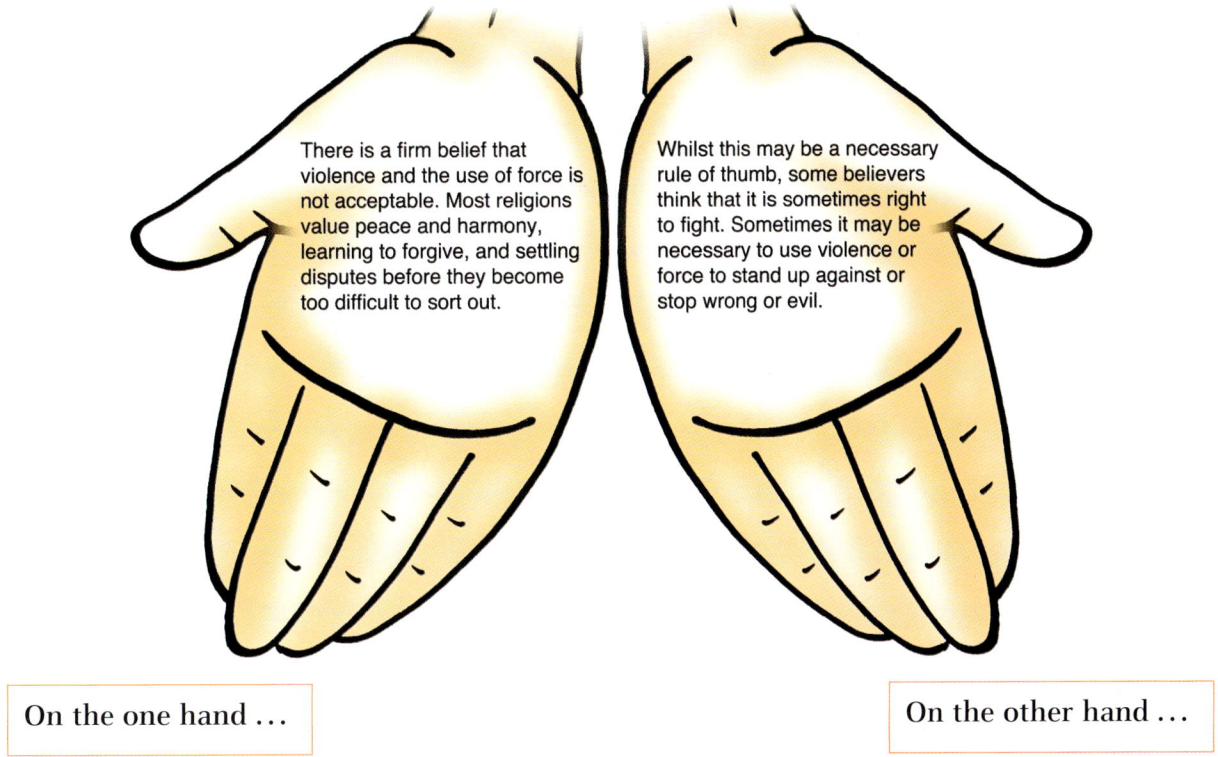

There is a firm belief that violence and the use of force is not acceptable. Most religions value peace and harmony, learning to forgive, and settling disputes before they become too difficult to sort out.

Whilst this may be a necessary rule of thumb, some believers think that it is sometimes right to fight. Sometimes it may be necessary to use violence or force to stand up against or stop wrong or evil.

On the one hand ...

On the other hand ...

But for many people it is left to their conscience.

Check it out

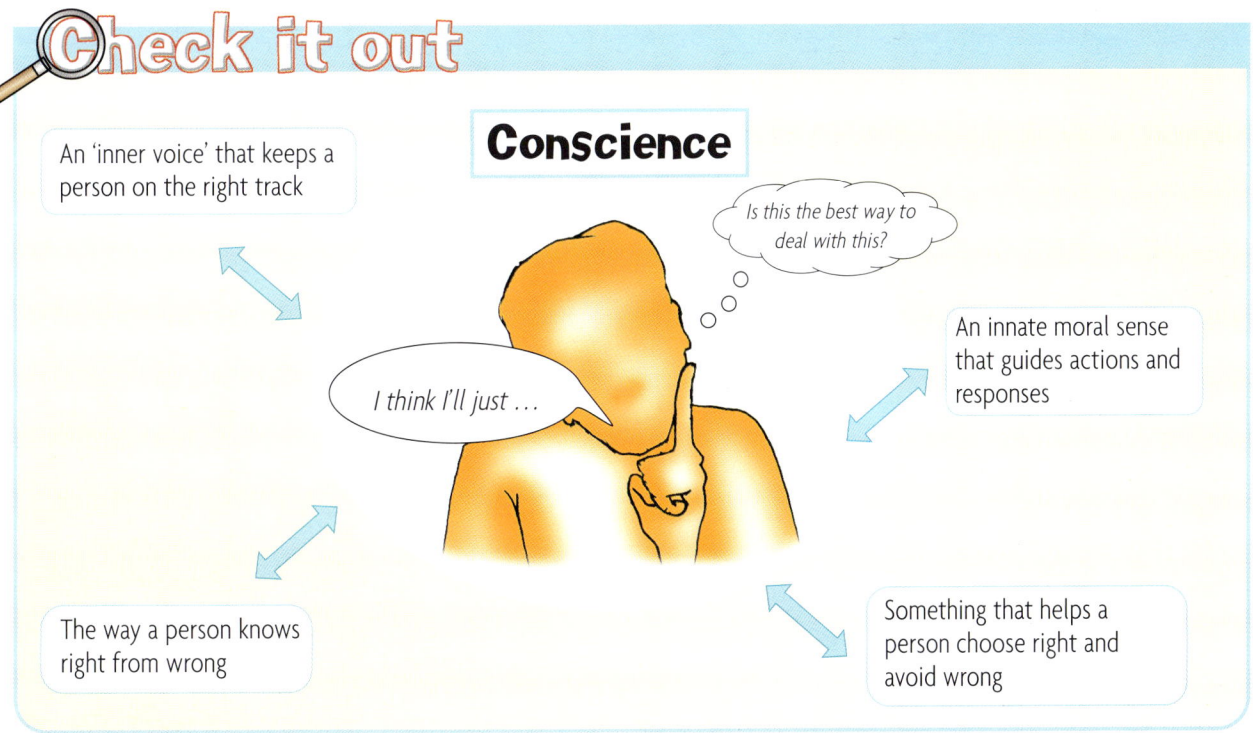

Conscience

An 'inner voice' that keeps a person on the right track

Is this the best way to deal with this?

I think I'll just ...

An innate moral sense that guides actions and responses

The way a person knows right from wrong

Something that helps a person choose right and avoid wrong

So what do religions teach about war and violence?

Some people say that religion is one of the causes of war and violence; they would give examples of conflict between groups with different religious backgrounds. To them, clashes between some Catholics and Protestants (Northern Ireland) or between some Christians and Muslims (Lebanon) or some Buddhists and Hindus (Sri Lanka) are just a few of the examples.

Sometimes such situations are not directly the result of the religion alone, but there may be political influences, issues to do with resources or rights, or responses to oppression and prejudice.

Many religions teach that, for the most part, violence and war is wrong; but some would add that there are circumstances when believers have to 'take up weapons', because not doing so would result in even more unacceptable situations.

In each religion there are sacred texts and teachings that believers will read and interpret when they are considering issues of conflict. Often within each tradition believers will differ in their opinions.

CHRISTIANITY ✞

'Greater love has no man than this, that a man lay down his life for his friends.'

John 15:13

INTERPRETATION:
Many Christians believe that it is sometimes necessary to go to war. St Augustine put forward the reasons which would justify Christians taking part in a war. These were later developed by St Thomas Aquinas into what has become known as the Just War theory. Many Christians today feel that when these conditions apply a war may be justified:
When there is a just cause.
When declared by a legitimate government.
When the motives are right.
When it is the last resort.
When the innocent are not harmed and the destruction is limited.
When there is a reasonable chance of success

'As long as the danger of war persists and there is no international authority with the necessary competence and power, governments cannot be denied the right of lawful self-defence, if all peace efforts have failed'.
   Catechism of the Catholic Church

For some Christians, defending and protecting others even at the cost of their own lives, may not only be justified but necessary.

Check it out

A war that can be justified according to agreed conditions

A war reluctantly taken on as a last resort and fought within limits

Just War

Is it for real	**J** ustice?
What	**U** ltimately results?
Who	**S** tarts it?
Has all else been	**T** ried?
Will there be a	**W** inner?
Can too much force be	**A** voided?
What is the	**R** eal aim?

A war that has to be fought to prevent a worse catastrophe

A war undertaken to protect the innocent or those being violated, and to restore justice and peace

---

'And behold, one of those who were with Jesus stretched out his hand and drew his sword, and struck the slave of the high priest, and cut off his ear. Then Jesus said to him, "Put your sword back into its place; for all who take the sword will perish by the sword."'

Matthew 26: 51–52

'Love your enemies and pray for your persecutors.'

Matthew 5.44

This means that many Quakers will refuse to join the army but act as Conscientious Objectors and work for disarmament.

Some Quakers are prepared to join medical corps and help those who become wounded.

INTERPRETATION:

Some Christians believe that the words and actions of Jesus show that Christians should not take part in any form of armed conflict. A commonly held belief amongst Quakers (Society of Friends) is that there is 'something of God' in all people and that Quakers should not try to harm them. For many Quakers a declaration made in 1660 has become a central part of their beliefs: *'We utterly deny all outward wars and strife, and fightings with outward weapons, for any end, or under any pretence.'*

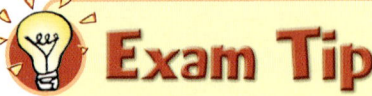

Using Stimuli to Help Evaluations.

On the exam paper there will be a number of pictures that will help you consider the questions. Look at the picture and consider the evaluation question before you begin the task.

Task

TASK ONE

● Having a religious belief cannot help you in times of war? Do you agree? Give reasons to support your answer showing you have thought about more than one point of view.

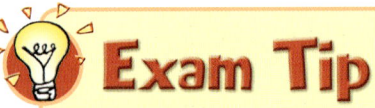

How to do Evaluative Questions

Try to follow the simple framework opposite when answering this type of question. This will ensure you meet the criteria in the Levels of Response Grid for AO3 questions, as shown on page 1.

W hat?	Ask yourself, 'What is the statement saying?'	*Read it carefully.*
A gree?	Say what you think for yourself. You can say, 'Yes, I agree' or 'No, I do not agree' or 'I partly agree and partly disagree.'	*Be clear and precise in what you say.*
W hy?	Give reasons and/or evidence to support your view. Try and include religious arguments or issues here if you can.	*Say why you have the view you have stated.*
O n the other hand?	Think about other views – not necessarily just the opposite view! Comment on them sensitively, and try to include religious ideas here if you haven't already done so.	*Make sure you consider other views or ideas.*
S o?	Round off your answer by coming to a conclusion, referring back to the statement in the question.	*End off with a clear conclusion to your answer.*

BUDDHISM ☸

'As a mother with her own life guards the life of her child, have all embracing thoughts for all that lives.'

Khuddaka Patha, Metta Sutta

INTERPRETATION:

Central to the Buddha's teachings in the Four Noble Truths and the Eightfold Path are the key beliefs of ahimsa (the principle of non-harming) and metta (friendliness or loving kindness). For Buddhists all life is interconnected and any action affects one's circumstances in this and future lives (kamma). Theravada Buddhists would say that killing is always wrong and brings kammic consequences.

For this reason many Buddhists will be pacifists and work in non-violent campaigns.

Mahayanna Buddhists, however, would say that if the motive is care for others and is done unselfishly, then it is not a wrong action.

HINDUISM ॐ

'Heroism, power, determination, resourcefulness, courage in battle, generosity and leadership are the qualities of work for the kshatriyas.'

Krishna's dialogue with Arjuna

Bhagavad Gita 18: 43

INTERPRETATION:

A central belief of Hinduism is ahimsa (non-violence) and Hindus are expected to work for peace. It is the dharma (main duty) of the kshatriyas to protect the innocent. The word 'kshatriya' means 'who protects from harm'. A true warrior will never hurt the innocent.

Armed conflict is allowed if it is to fight against evil and prevents something worse happening.

ISLAM

'And fight in the cause of God those who fight with you, but do not go over the limits; God does not love the aggressors.'

Surah 2: 190

INTERPRETATION:

The greater Jihad is the personal struggle against all the temptations to do wrong and act against the wishes of Allah. There are clear conditions for military war (the lesser jihad) but the main aim should be to restore peace and freedom.

Fighting should only be used in defence; it should be the last resort; it should be led by a spiritual leader and civilians, trees, crops and animals should be protected.

'Permission to fight is given to those who are attacked, because they have been wronged. Allah has power to help them. They are those who have been unjustly driven from their homes, only because they said: "Our Lord is Allah."'

Surah 22: 39–40

'If two parties of believers quarrel, make peace between them. If either of them commits aggression against the other, fight against the aggressors until they submit to Allah's judgement. When they submit, make peace between them with justice and be fair. Allah loves those who are fair.'

Surah 49:9

JUDAISM

'You shall not slay them. Would you slay those whom you have taken captive with your sword and with your bow? Set bread and water before them, that they may eat and drink and go to their master.'

2 Kings 6:22

INTERPRETATION:

Jews regard peace as the ideal state and so the Messianic age is seen in terms of one of peaceful harmony. When warfare happens then it is important to treat those captured justly.

'He shall judge between many peoples, and shall decide for strong nations afar off; and they shall beat their swords into ploughshares, and their spears into pruning hooks; nation shall not lift up sword against nation, neither shall there be war anymore.'

Micah 4:3

Many Jews accept that sometimes wars have to happen but within the Jewish community there are many examples of projects that seek peace and interfaith dialogue.

SIKHISM

'Those who beat you with fists, do not give them blows. Go to their homes yourself and kiss their feet.'

Guru Granth Sahib

INTERPRETATION:

Conflict should always be a last resort. In 1699 Guru Gobind Singh called upon Sikhs to become members of the Khalsa. He fought in defensive battles and said when all other means have failed it is permissible to draw the sword. Dharam Yodh (war in defence of righteousness) sets out the principles for when a Sikh should become involved in a war.

It must be a last resort with no wish for revenge. The army should be made up of soldiers committed to the cause with a minimum of force being necessary. Any land or property captured during war should be returned afterwards.

Within many religious traditions there are people who are against all forms of war and use of force or violence. They are often called 'pacifists' – because they believe peace is always the best aim and approach. Such people would refuse to participate in any fighting, even if their government conscripts them into the armed forces. During the war, they were called 'conscientious objectors' – because they objected to taking part in the war on grounds of conscience.

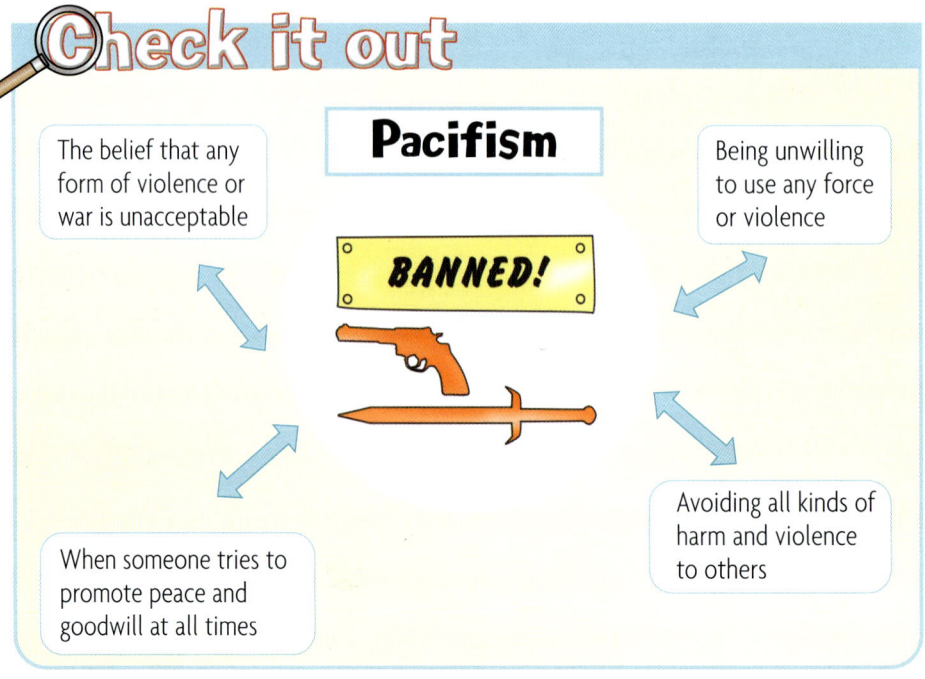

Check it out

Pacifism

The belief that any form of violence or war is unacceptable

Being unwilling to use any force or violence

BANNED!

Avoiding all kinds of harm and violence to others

When someone tries to promote peace and goodwill at all times

Peace and reconciliation
Ways of keeping peace

GLOBALLY

United Nations

Founded in 1945 it is an association of states working together for peace and security. By making nations think globally not nationally it actively seeks ways to develop friendly relations among countries and settle differences by peaceful means.

Look it up
http://www.un.org/

ECUMENICALLY

Corrymeela

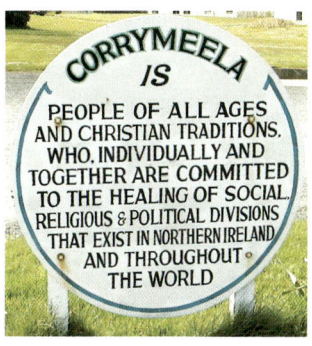

During the years of conflict between Protestants and Roman Catholics in Northern Ireland the Christian Community of Corrymeela has provided a base for both sides to come together. Its name means 'Hill of Harmony'.

Look it up
http://www.corrymeela.org/

INTERFAITH

Neve Shalom/Wahat al-Salam

Neve Shalom/Wahat Al-Salam (an oasis of peace) is an area in Israel where Jewish and Arab families live together in peaceful co-existence. It holds many activities where Jewish and Arab children play and learn together.

Look it up
http://nswas.com

Ways of Avoiding War

Although organisations can play a vital role in promoting and maintaining peace, many methods can start from just one person taking a non-violent role, and having an effect on others.

Martin Luther King

As a Baptist minister influenced by the teachings of love from Jesus:

- Used non-violent protest to support civil rights for black Americans;
- Staged sit-ins and protest marches;
- Went to jail for his actions;
- Made many speeches;
- Was awarded the Nobel Peace Prize in 1964.

Look it up

http://martinlutherking.8m.com

Leonard Bird

As a Quaker he used the Peace Testimony;

- Opposed war and became a conscientious objector;
- Visited Russia to promote contacts between people;
- Imprisoned three times for his anti-war protest.

Look it up

http://www.ppu.org.uk

Nichadatsu Fujii

- After the bombing of Hiroshima and Nagasaki, Nichadatsu Fujii dedicated his life to the wonderful law of the Lotus-Flower Sutra.
- As a Buddhist he campaigned for peace by conducting peace marches.
- Actively supported the construction of Peace Pagodas throughout the world.

Look it up

http://www.spiritofchange.org
www.web.mit.edu/stclair/www/
pagoda/html

Mahatma Gandhi

- Hindu believer and activist for Ahimsa;
- Used non-violence in the protest against British rule in India, e.g. burning of passes;
- Led marches, fasts and was imprisoned for his activities;
- Lived life as an example of Satyagraha

Look it up

http://www.mkgandhi.org

Bashir al-Khayi

- Reconciled with Dalia Landau, a person who had settled in his house.
- Co-founded Open House Peace Centre to support co-existence of Muslims and Jews in Palestine.

Look it up

http://www.openhouse.org.il/
healing/shtml

Leo Baeck

- Refused ways of escape when Nazis came to power;
- Continued to support civic rights of Jews;
- Sent to concentration camp;
- After his release he worked for interfaith dialogue.

Look it up

http://www.wbenjamin.org/baeckhtml

Bhai Kanhaya

- As a water carrier in the battle of Anandpur he gave water to the enemy on the battlefield;
- Guru Gobind Singh called him a 'true Sikh' because of his actions.

Look it up

http://www.punjabilok.com/faith/sikh/gurugobind.htm

http://www.sgpc.net/photo-gallery/photogallery6.html

Task

- Find out about information of another individual in the religions you have studied who has shown the importance of harmony or non-violence in their actions.

Many believers who are pacifists would say that it is possible to protest about such things in a non-violent way.

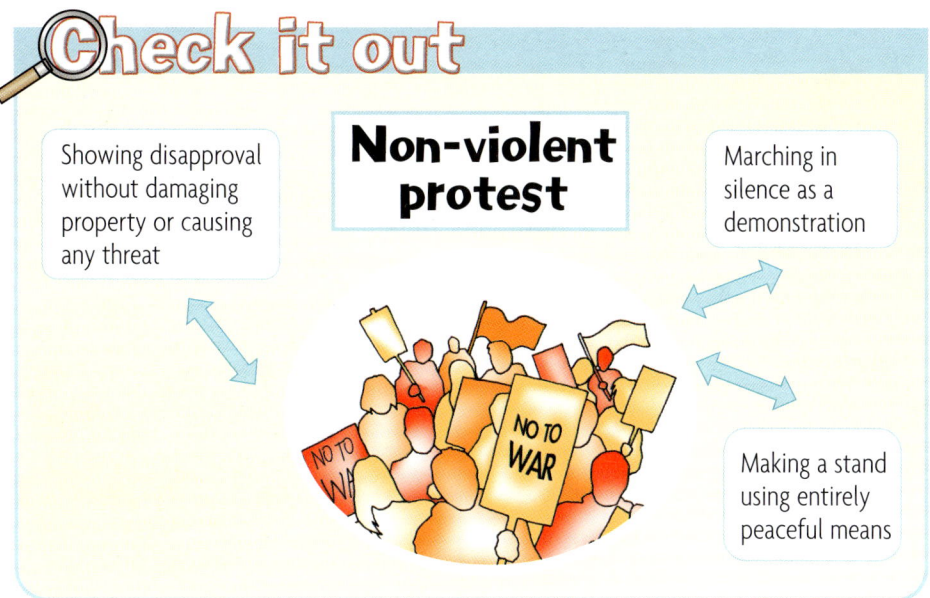

Check it out

Non-violent protest

Showing disapproval without damaging property or causing any threat

Marching in silence as a demonstration

Making a stand using entirely peaceful means

Ways of learning to forgive

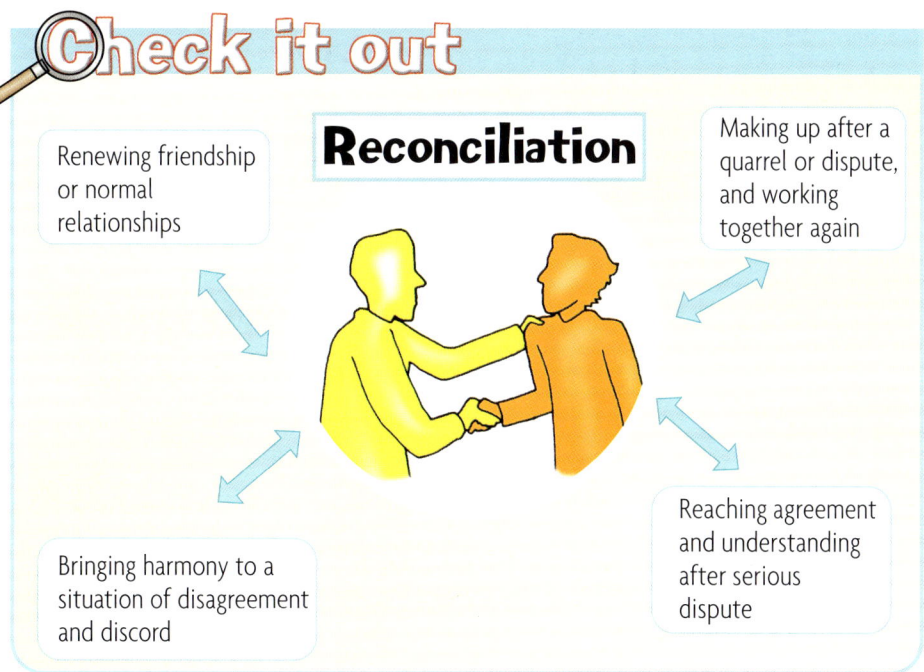

Check it out

Reconciliation

Renewing friendship or normal relationships

Making up after a quarrel or dispute, and working together again

Bringing harmony to a situation of disagreement and discord

Reaching agreement and understanding after serious dispute

Most religions emphasize the importance and need for forgiveness. It is often seen as the major way of absorbing the wrong and evil we meet in our lives; by not responding to it in like manner, but repaying good for the evil and wrong, and forgiving the one who perpetrated the evil against us.

Exam Tip

Within the work of this course you will sometimes be expected to give an example or describe the work of a person or an organisation, or give an example. In this unit you will be expected to know about one individual and the way they used or commended a non-violent approach. When answering questions make sure that the details you give are relevant to the unit, and to the particular aspect. Use the IMPACT framework to help you.

Task

- Select one person who has used or campaigned for non-violence. Complete the following framework to describe the IMPACT of their work and example.

I	dentify ...	the correct name of the person
M	ention ...	the religious tradition to which they belong
P	récis ...	the context in which they worked
A	cknowledge ...	some of the main aspects of their work or example
C	onsider ...	how their example demonstrates the teachings of the religious tradition to which they belong
T	ell ...	of specific actions or projects that relate to their work and beliefs.

Each religion has clear teachings about the importance of forgiveness.

- The Teachings of Jesus e.g. The Beatitudes; his words from the cross
- The actions of Jesus e.g. Zacchaeus
- Examples of Christians forgiving e.g. Martin Luther King
- The Lord's Prayer

- The teachings of the Buddha concerning Metta
- The second and third of the six perfections
- The actions of the Buddha e.g. when he met Angulimala

- Examples of Hindus e.g. Gandhi's practice and sayings
- Dharma

FORGIVE ONE ANOTHER

- Example of Guru Nanak
- Consistent with the emphasis of overcoming one's ego and being like God
- Adi Granth 1378 – If someone hits you, do not hit him back. Go home – after kissing his feet

- Teachings from the Tenakh e.g. treatment of enemies
- Importance of repentance (teshuvah)
- Role of Rosh Hashanah and the ten days of returning
- Only the victim can forgive

- The example of Muhammad
- Rules of War
- Teachings from the Qur'an e.g. those who forgive others will be rewarded by Allah (Surah 42.40)
- The belief that Allah will always forgive someone who is truly penitent

Ways to rebuild bridges

Whenever there has been conflict, or violence, or war, there is always a need to rebuild relationships afterwards. There can be no success unless, after the hostility, and the forgiveness, there is a process of rebuilding and making new.

This is true in relationships between people, when a dispute and difference has come between them, there needs to be forgiveness and a rebuilding of trust and openness between the two people.

Likewise, when communities are involved in conflict and serious disputes, there has to be a process of rebuilding the community and its positive relationships after the forgiveness has been offered and received.

Each year prizes are given for women building peace and preventing violent conflict. Fiona Brovina founded the league of Albanian Woman which protested against the war, and took care of women, children and the elderly. She said her only weapons were her pen and her stethoscope.

TEST IT OUT

Here is a typical set of examination questions for this unit. Write out answers to them, trying to take account of the Exam Tips and information you have been given.

(a) State **two** issues that can cause conflict. [2]

(b) What is pacifism? [2]

(c) 'Love your enemies and pray for those who persecute you.' (Matthew 5:44) Explain why Christians might want to put this teaching into practice. [4]

(d) Explain the importance of forgiveness in the teachings of **one** religious tradition. [4]

(e) Describe from **two** different religious traditions the teachings about taking part in a war. [6]

(f) 'Religions can't help to rebuild peace. Only governments can.' Do you agree? Give reasons or evidence for your answer, showing that you have thought about more than one point of view. [6]

2 Religion and Medicine

The Big Picture

Rights of the unborn child – Whose Choice Is It?

Should people have freewill to make life/death decisions?

Is there anything medicine can't do?

How far should we go in defending and promoting life?

Questions to ask

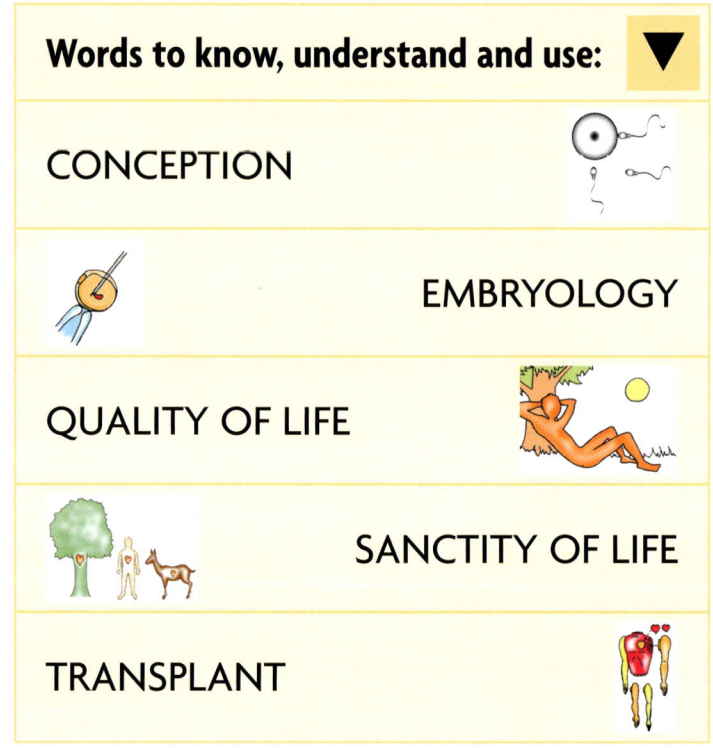

Words to know, understand and use: ▼

CONCEPTION

EMBRYOLOGY

QUALITY OF LIFE

SANCTITY OF LIFE

TRANSPLANT

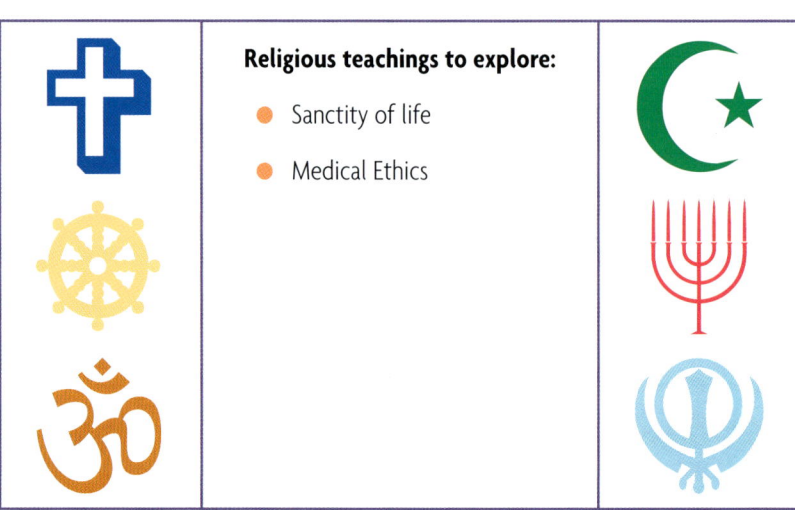

Religious teachings to explore:

● Sanctity of life

● Medical Ethics

Should people have freewill to make life/death decisions?

'I don't agree with all this intervention of science — it's like playing God.'

'Life is not held sacred anymore. People forget about the santity of life.'

'When I think of the suffering my aunt went through I realised it doesn't matter how long you live — it's the quality of life that matters.'

'A baby is a human being from the moment of conception. I don't believe in abortion.'

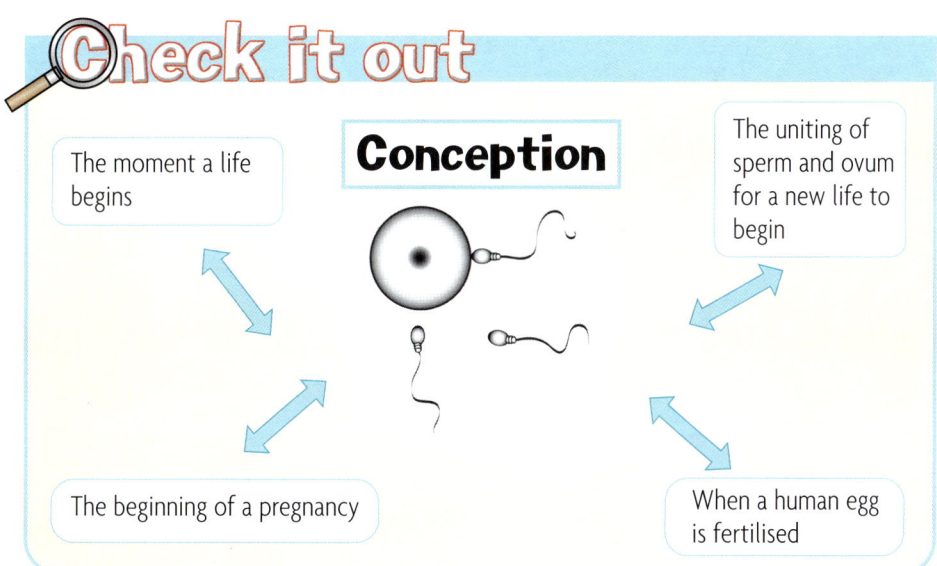

Check it out

Conception

The moment a life begins

The uniting of sperm and ovum for a new life to begin

The beginning of a pregnancy

When a human egg is fertilised

Check it out

Quality of Life

When a person feels of value and capable of contributing to life

The extent to which life is meaningful and pleasurable

Feeling valued and on top of the world!

Being free from undue pain, anxiety and stress

Check it out

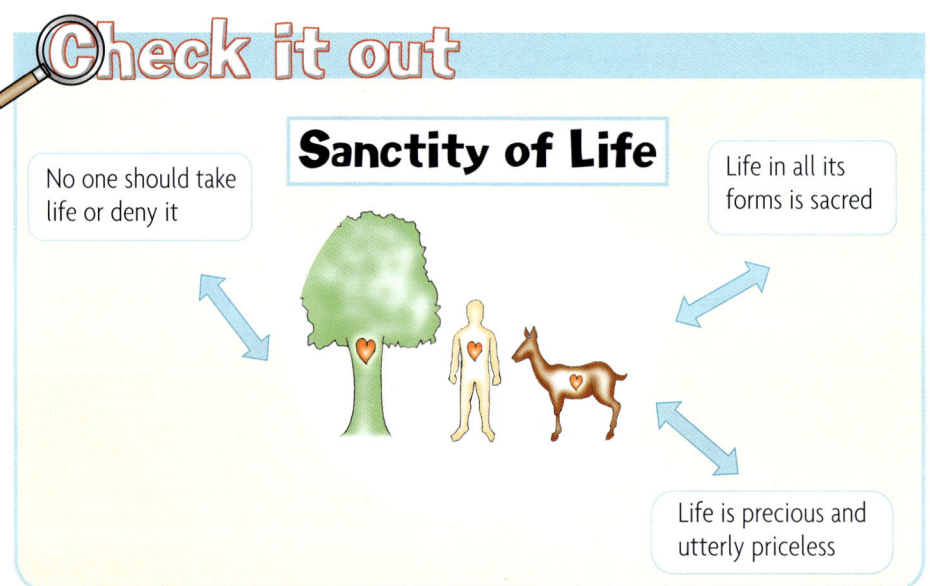

Sanctity of Life

No one should take life or deny it

Life in all its forms is sacred

Life is precious and utterly priceless

 **Exam Tip**

When giving an answer that requires a definition, be precise in what you say. Many candidates do not gain full marks because they repeat words or phrases within their answer, or because they do not cover the essential points of a definition.

Q *What is meant by 'the sanctity of life'?* [2]

Look at the answers below, and you will see a full answer and a part answer;

Answer A	Answer B
sacredness	The belief that all life is sacred, and therefore precious; so valuable that no one should take that life away.

Religious teachings on the Sanctity of Life

Sanctity of Life in Christianity ✝	Sanctity of Life in Buddhism ☸	Sanctity of Life in Hinduism ॐ
• God is interested and involved in each human's life • Life is sacred and a gift from God • Only God should take life away • Jesus showed in his teaching that all life should be valued	• From the moment of conception an embryo is a living being • All forms of life are caught in the cycle of existence (samsara), and are affected by actions and their karma (kamma) • Being born as a human is a very precious thing, and has the potential for completion and nirvana	• The soul is present in all species of life • All life is sacred and worthy of the highest respect • Everything that lives and grows is interconnected • Where there is life or soul there is atman • At death the soul enters another body

Sanctity of Life in Islam ☪	Sanctity of Life in Judaism 🕎	Sanctity of Life in Sikhism ☬
• Every soul has been created by Allah • Allah has a plan for each life • No one has the right to take their own or anyone else's life	• Life is sacred and a gift from God • *Pukuach nefesh* shows the importance of putting aside laws to save life	• Life is sacred, and should never be violated • Life begins at conception

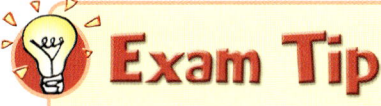 **Exam Tip**

You must include specific religious content in your answers to questions about the teachings or practices of religious traditions, even though it seems easier to write about more general cultural traditions or understandings.

 Explain why many religious believers see life as sacred. [4]

Look at the answer below. It has been given a Level 2 and two marks. What would you change or add to it to make it a Level 4 and four marks?

> Many believers see life as sacred because God created everything that there is, so it belongs to him. This means all life is very precious, and should not be wasted.

27

Whose choice is it?

To many people the issue of abortion is to do with choice and rights:

- The choices and rights of the mother, and whether she wants and is able to have the baby
- The rights of the child not yet born, to be alive and grow independently
- The choice about making decisions in accordance with one's own conscience
- The right of religious believers to consider how their beliefs impact on such an issue.

Deciding what to do as a believer

CHRISTIANITY

- There is no single Christian view on abortion, and individual Christians differ in their response, sometimes even with the 'official stance' of their particular denomination
- Generally, Christians do have concerns about abortion, because of their beliefs in:
  - The sanctity of life
  - People being in the image of God
  - That all life – whatever form – is precious and purposeful, and so sacred
- Roman Catholic Churches and Orthodox Churches generally forbid abortion under any circumstances, because they believe that life is sacred and God-given
- Other Christian churches tend to be against abortion carried out for social reasons, but accept that in some instances, it may be a preferred choice (such as when having to decide between the life of the mother or the child)
- Many Evangelical Protestants are supporters of a Pro-Life stance, and would tend to be against abortion in principle, although acknowledge that there are some specific circumstances which may make it allowable
- Many Christian denominations leave it open to individual Christians to determine for themselves whether or not abortion is right in their own particular circumstances

CASE STUDY

Sioned is 18, and is working in a company that produces medicines and treatments for chemists and hospitals.

1. She has done well since leaving school
2. She hopes to continue and get promotion
3. She has a steady boyfriend, David
4. They hope one day to marry
5. David is at university
6. He is studying religion and hopes to become a teacher.

Sioned has just discovered she is pregnant, and is trying to decide what to do. She and David are both believers. Sioned is thinking of having an abortion, and is wondering whether their religion would let them do so. She writes to a problem page in a magazine to ask for help.

BUDDHISM

- No human should be killed, and this includes the foetus
- An exception would be when the pregnancy is a source of intense suffering for some members of the family, or when the mother's life is at risk, or the life of the child is going to be seriously handicapped
- The Five Precepts should be used as guiding principles, and so each individual must make their own decision about their own circumstances
- Abortion can be seen as breaking the First Precept, as it is a cutting off a 'precious human rebirth', which is seen as beginning at conception
- Bad karma from an abortion is said to vary according to the size of the foetus
- Some groups, motivated by the principle of compassion, do attach a particular significance to birth

SIKHISM

- Abortion is morally wrong, because life begins at conception
- The sanctity of life should never be violated
- Conception following rape is regarded by some as a possible justification for an abortion
- A child likely to be born deformed is not usually regarded as sufficient grounds for an abortion, although some Sikhs do recognise the right of parents to decide for themselves in this situation

HINDUISM

- All life is sacred and there should be no interference in natural processes
- The source of all life forms is God, and so should be treated with the highest respect
- Abortion is against ahimsa (harmlessness)
- Some would allow abortion for strict medical reasons (i.e. saving the life of the mother)
- Some believe that the foetus has no shape or personality until the fifth month of pregnancy, so can be aborted before if there are good reasons
- Others would argue that it is an acceptable method of ending unwanted pregnancy, and therefore is a kind of birth control; recognising the legality of abortions in India, as long as they take place in Government clinics

JUDAISM

- God is the creator, and he alone can take life
- Life is God's greatest gift, and it should be preserved – a priority over all else
- Destroying a life is therefore a heinous crime
- Abortion is permitted in some circumstances, such as saving the life of the mother
- Some Jews would also see abortion as allowable in cases of rape, incest, or perhaps even when the general health of the mother was poor

What do you think?

Is there an answer?

Can religious teaching help – or does it just make it more difficult?

Task

a)

Look at each of the points 1–6. In pairs order them to show which would have most importance in making a decision.

b)

Write a 'problem page' answer to Sioned for each of the religious traditions you are studying.

What would you advise someone in this situation to do? And what reasons would you give?

ISLAM

- Life is seen to be sacred, and not disposable, except for just causes
- Allah creates all life, and only he can end it
- Abortion for purely economic reasons is forbidden in the Qur'an
- Many do allow abortion if the mother's life is at stake
- Some will also allow abortion if the child to be born is likely to be seriously deformed or diseased – although others reject this as a just cause
- The taking of the life of a child is seen as sin, and in the next life, young children at judgement will have the right to know why they were killed
- Up to four months after conception the mother's rights are greater than those of the child; after 4 months the child has equal rights with the mother
- 120 days after conception 'ensoulment' (receiving of the soul) takes place, therefore some would forbid abortions after this stage
- There is a purpose in suffering, and no expectation that life will be enjoyable/easy
- At judgement, Allah will take into account a person's intention (niyyah) in the act

Exam Tip

Many views seem the same. Check out the similarities and differences between the two religious traditions you are studying. Remember to be specific in your answers – do not use a 'cover all' type of answer.

Task

- When you have written your 'problem page' answers from two different religious traditions, list the arguments that are the same, and those that are different from the two religious traditions.

Q *Explain the attitude of **two** different religious traditioins to abortion.* [6]

Task

● Correct this answer:

Both the religions I study are against abortion because it is God who gives life, and God who should take it. So they do not agree with abortions.

Personal and Public Debate

As with many issues, it is not always simply a matter of making up your own mind – there are other people's views to consider:

'But what about us? We don't believe it is right to take away a life!'

'Hang on a minute – it's partly my child too. I'm sure we can work something out together.'

'You need to think of the long-term effects of an abortion, as well as what seems important now.'

'As a neighbour, I think she should just make up her own mind! She's the one who'll have the baby anyway.'

'I want to stand by my sister; but I really hate the idea of her having an abortion.'

'It's my choice. I can't have a baby now – it will ruin my career.'

'As your religious leader, I urge you to consider the principles of the sanctity of life before reaching a decision.'

So how does a believer decide when there is no specific teaching in religious traditions about modern medical issues?

Most religious traditions would probably expect believers to use some of the following methods to arrive at a sensible and acceptable conclusion:

Search the sacred texts for references or beliefs that may relate to the issue

Think about ultimate principles in the religion that will have an impact on the issue

Analyse intentions, and measure them against other relevant teachings

How do believers decide what is right in modern medical ethics?

Discuss the matter with other believers, and with 'experts' in the religion and the issue

Pray about the issues involved and seek guidance directly from God

Consider the effects on themselves and others, and on society as a whole, and weigh up whether these are compatible with basic beliefs

31

Is there anything medicine cannot do?

As science develops there are many more scientific advancements in the creation and saving of life. Each individual will make their own decisions but these will often be influenced by the teachings of any religious tradition to which they belong.

When you look in a newspaper, you can see examples of the many ways that science is defending and promoting the right to live from cradle to grave.

IVF
(In-vitro-fertilisation)

The egg of the woman is fertilised outside the womb using either the husband's or a donor's sperm, and then replaced in the womb.

For many couples it may be difficult for them to have babies. Up to 10% of couples in the United Kingdom have to get medical help in order to have a baby.

There are many different examples of solutions produced by medical technology known as **Embryo Technology**.

In some cases an egg is donated by another woman and is fertilised by IVF using the husband's sperm, and then it is inserted into the womb.

Embryo donation is when both the egg and the sperm come from donors, and are fertilised outside of the womb, and then placed inside to allow it to develop and grow.

DAILY BUGLE
20p

THANKS TO IVF TECHNOLOGY, A 56-YEAR OLD WOMAN IS PREGNANT WITH TWINS. SHOULD SHE BE?

DAILY BUGLE

20p

IS THIS INTERFERING IN NATURE?

AIH
(Artificial Insemination by Husband)

When the husband's sperm is inserted into his wife's womb by a medical procedure.

This is used when the couple have difficulty in conceiving, but where the sperm and ovum are normally fine.

AID
(Artificial Insemination by Donor)

When an anonymous man donates sperm, which is then inserted into the womb of a woman by a medical procedure.

This is used when a couple have difficulty conceiving because of problems with the husband's sperm.

DAILY BUGLE

20p

WILL THE DONOR BE OF THE SAME RELIGION?

Surrogacy

When the egg and sperm, of wife and husband are fertilised by IVF (outside the womb) and then inserted into another woman's womb; or, when another woman is artificially inseminated by the husband's sperm.

In both cases, after the birth the woman (surrogate mother) hands the baby to the husband and wife.

This method is used when the couple have difficulty conceiving because of problems with either the woman's eggs, or with her womb not being able to keep a foetus for long enough.

DAILY BUGLE

20p

IS THIS GOING AGAINST GOD'S WILL?

Some questions to be asked:

- Is this playing God?
- What happens to the other embryos?
- When does life begin?

A New Approach to Family Planning

In about 15 years time it will not be unusual for a single woman to freeze her eggs. Then when she has a firm foothold in her career, has met Mr Right and feels ready to start a family, she will have one of her eggs thawed, fertilised with her partner's sperm, and the embryo implanted for pregnancy. A year or so later she can do the same again, or whenever it is convenient for her to have another child. Under the Human Rights Act she will be entitled to do this free.

- Should there be an age restriction?
- Is it murder if the other embryos are destroyed?
- Is technology being abused?
- What if Mr Right is never found?

Task

- Answer two of the questions above giving reasons or evidence for your answers

Check it out

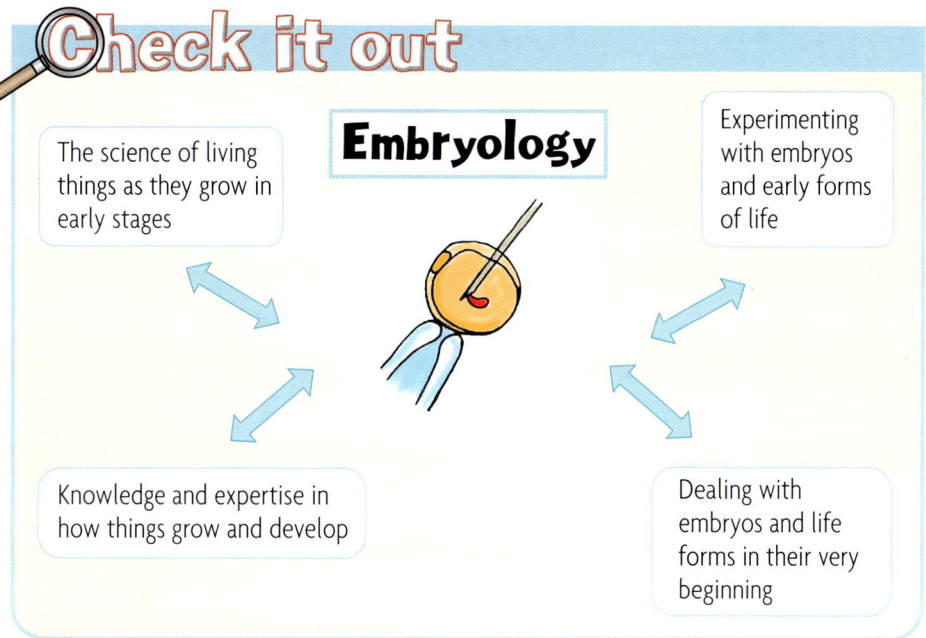

Embryology

The science of living things as they grow in early stages

Experimenting with embryos and early forms of life

Knowledge and expertise in how things grow and develop

Dealing with embryos and life forms in their very beginning

Check it out

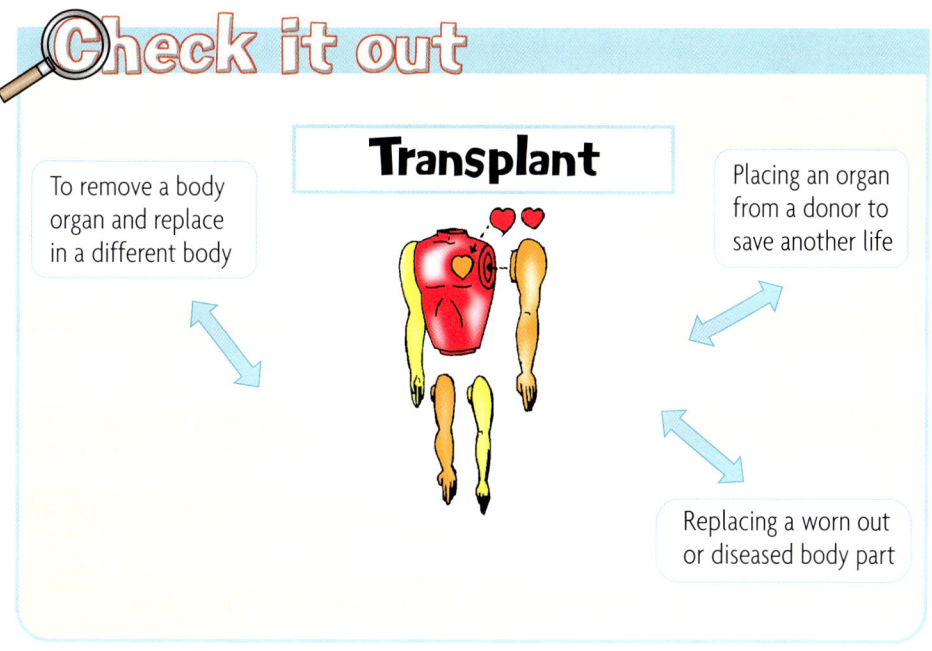

Transplant

To remove a body organ and replace in a different body

Placing an organ from a donor to save another life

Replacing a worn out or diseased body part

What do religions teach about medical ethics?

CHRISTIANITY

Some very different views, but all would often promote adoption.

Roman Catholic:
Life is given by God and no one has a right to children. All embryo technology is banned for Catholics because:

- IVF involves throwing away some of the fertilised eggs
- Children have a right to know who their parents are
- Fertilisation takes place apart from the sex act, but God intended procreation to be a part of the sex act
- Pope Pius XII states that third party IVF is adultery

Other Christian Denominations:
Some would accept the first three bullet points above and would also accept IVF, but wish to point out:

- It provides happiness to the couple
- Technology is also God's gift, but may be abused
- Will the cost be justifiable when so many children are starving?

BUDDHISM

- There is no infallible authority which a Buddhist has to accept
- Consideration should be made of the five precepts which states no harm to any living being

HINDUISM

- Law of Manu encourages infertile couples to adopt a relative
- AIH and IVF are acceptable as they use sperm and egg from husband and wife
- The discarded embryos are not foetuses as no soul has been transferred to them
- AID and embryo donation are not allowed as caste is passed down through the father

DEFINITIONS

IVF

Fertilising of the egg outside of the womb.

Surrogacy

Implanting of couple's fertilised egg, or insemination of donor egg in a volunteer woman.

Cloning

Copying an embryo and all its characteristics to produce an identical birth.

AIH/AID

Implanting sperm from husband or donor.

Genetic Engineering

Making change to an embryo's structure to prevent disability or disease.

JUDAISM

- Egg should be donated by a Jewish woman so the child is Jewish

- AID can be seen as a form of adultery and children have a right to know who their parents are

- Importance of having children is stressed in the tradition

ISLAM

- Many accept AIH and IVF because the egg and sperm are from the husband and wife

- It is considered important to know who the natural parents are

- IVF allowed under special circumstances, such as if a male has a disease

- Qur'an warns that the semen or sperm should not be destroyed or wasted

SIKHISM

- Some believe that these areas are likely to be tampering with the natural body God has given, and are wrong

- Some believe that using God-given knowledge and skill is important and should be used to help those with disorders

- AID is wrong, and is a form of adultery; AIH and IVF (when only couples sperm and ovum used) is acceptable

- Surrogacy is not acceptable; being willing to accept childlessness, or to adopt children is preferred

Task

- Use the writing frame below to make links and describe connections on the religious teachings and their impact on the issues so far described in this unit. Write one on each of the religious traditions you are studying, and do *either* the same issue in both, *or* do a different issue for each of the religious traditions.

There are many ways that science can help in the creation of life. Two ways are through the use of .... and .... One of the religious traditions I have studied .... believes that science can help in the creation of life when .... In the other religious traditions I have studied .... many believers consider that

....

Before making a decision the believer may consult .... to see what their religion teaches on the matter. As few sacred books refer to scientific advancements in the creation of life, they will often ask people to help them .... the sacred texts.

WORD BANK
Some of the words here may help you in your answers:
Sacred texts; abortion; I.V.F; Euthanasia; Cloning; A.I.D; Embryo Technology; Interpretation; Organ Transplants; Organ Removal; Life-support technology; priests; quality of life.

How far should we go in defending and promoting life?

Medical science has developed rapidly, and today it is possible to cure or help people to survive illnesses or accidents that at one time would have been fatal.

But such advances also bring dilemmas or at least a series of questions, not just in questions to do with the beginning of life, but also in other areas of medical practice, such as:

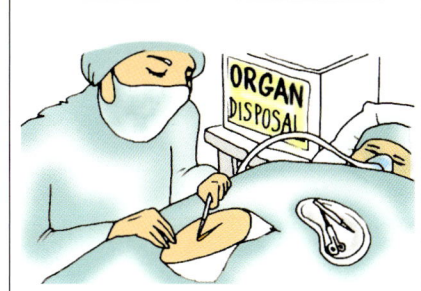

Organ Transplants

Organ Removal

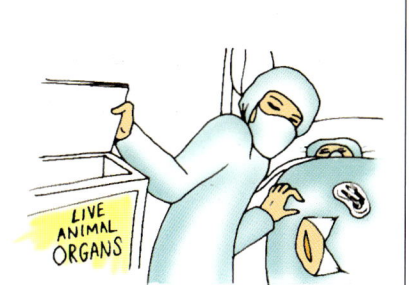

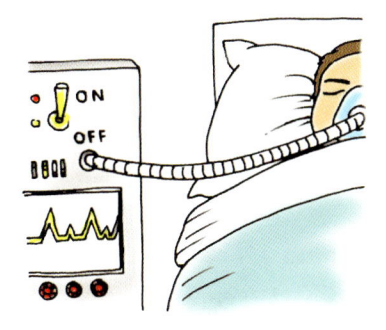

Keeping Alive

Life-Support Technology

Cloning

Withdrawing life support

Commandment?
Life is ....
Objectives?
Not unique
Individuals valued
No experimentation
God's will and plan?

In these areas, questions arise that believers have to answer in the light of their beliefs about life, their beliefs about God (or the Ultimate Being), and their beliefs about death and any afterlife.

For example:

Is this interfering with nature or God's plan?

Should the overriding issue be the preservation of life?

To what extent is it sacrilege to use human tissues or organs in human beings?

Is this trying to be God?

Is the quality of life as important as the maintaining of it?

Can it ever be justified to use an organ from a dead person to preserve someone elses' life?

Is life meant to go on forever?

Should anyone have the responsibility to switch off a life support machine?

TEST IT OUT

(a) State **two** ways science can help save lives. [2]

(b) What is *embryology?* [2]

(c) Why do many religious people believe life is sacred? [4]

(d) Explain **two** considerations doctors may make when withdrawing life-support technology. [4]

(e) Explain the teachings of **two** different religious traditions towards organ transplants. [6]

(f) 'It's the quality of life that matters – not how long you live.' Do you agree? Give reasons or evidence for your answer showing that you have thought about more than one point of view. [6]

3 Religious Expression

The Big Picture

Questions to ask

Why worship in special buildings?

How do people express their interests?

How does pilgrimage help a person's spiritual growth?

How do people share their faith?

Words to know, understand and use: ▼
SACRED
HOLY
PILGRIMAGE
SYMBOLISM
INTERFAITH DIALOGUE

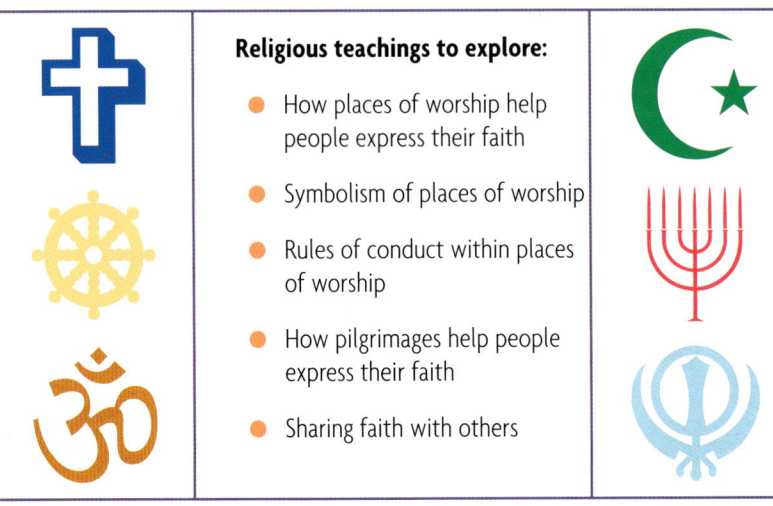

Religious teachings to explore:

- How places of worship help people express their faith
- Symbolism of places of worship
- Rules of conduct within places of worship
- How pilgrimages help people express their faith
- Sharing faith with others

How do people express their interest in something?

I'm interested in ...

What are you interested in? How do you show it?

We all have ways that show we are interested in things — it might be going to a special place or event; learning more about something; talking to people who share the same interests; or joining with other people in a project of some kind. Can you think of others?

Why worship in special buildings?

For people of a religious faith, one of the ways of expressing their faith is by going to a place of worship.

The purpose of a building is likely to show in the way it is designed. Think about the different purposes between a school and a cinema, and how they are designed to suit their particular purpose.

In the same way, a place designed for worship will have particular requirements and features. Look at all the jigsaw pieces below, and decide which would make a place conducive to, or more helpful for worship, and explain how.

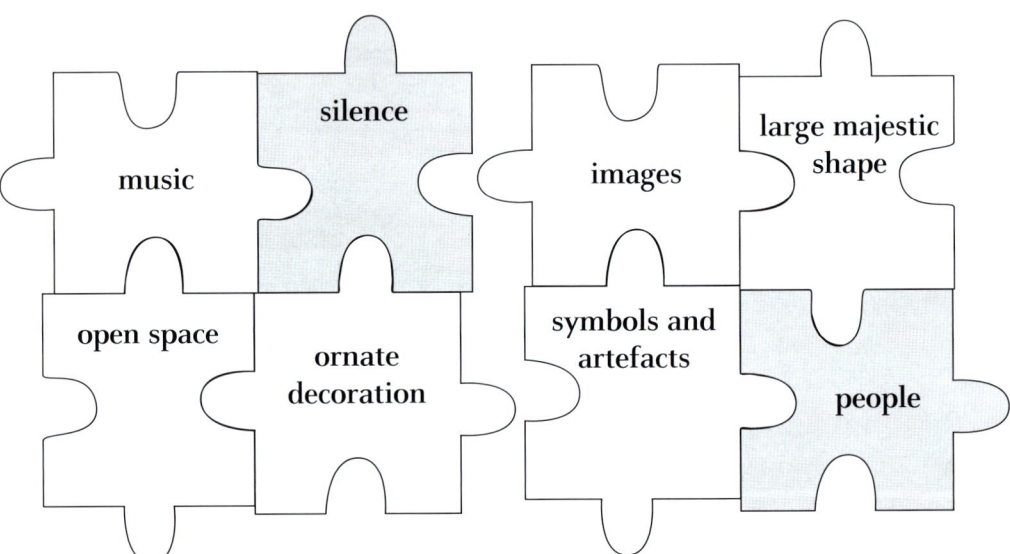

music

silence

large majestic shape

images

open space

ornate decoration

symbols and artefacts

people

Can you think of others?

Check it out

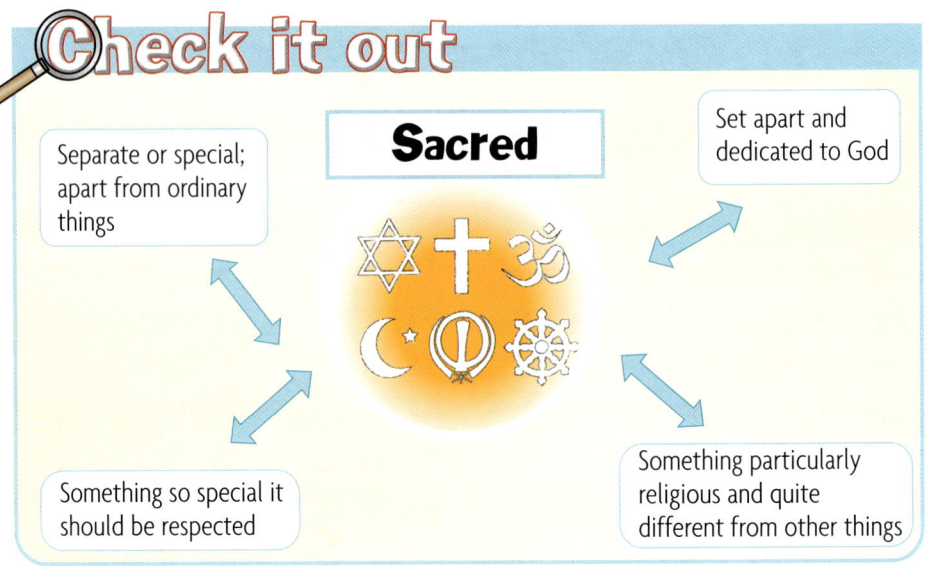

Separate or special; apart from ordinary things

Sacred

Set apart and dedicated to God

Something so special it should be respected

Something particularly religious and quite different from other things

Check it out

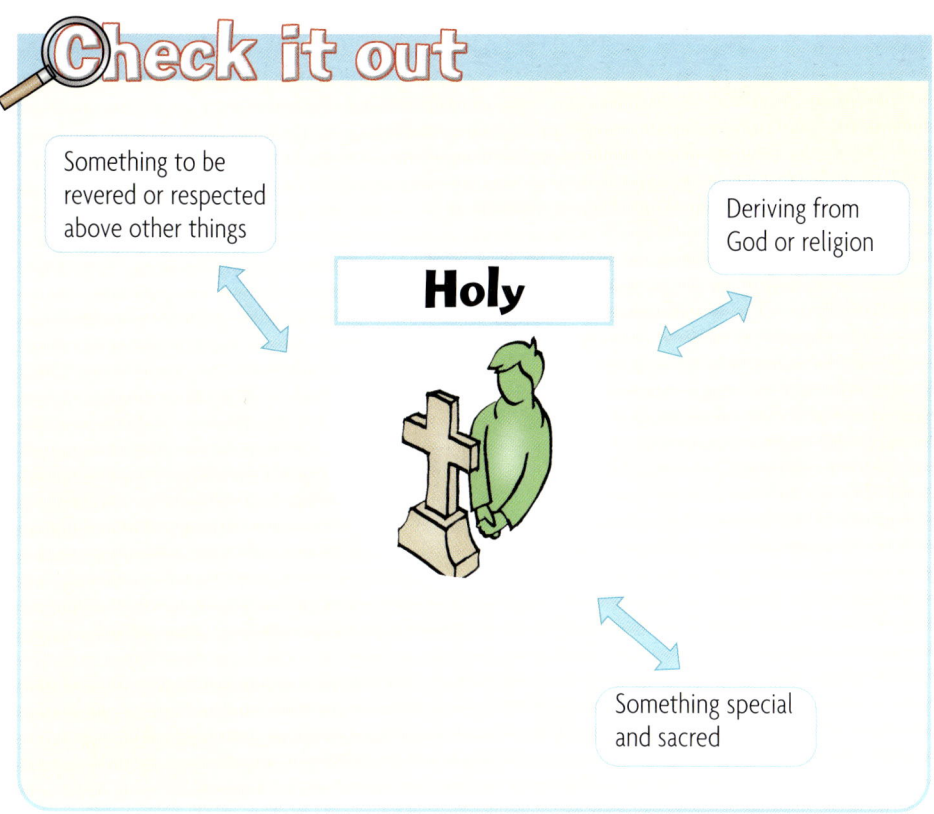

Something to be revered or respected above other things

Holy

Deriving from God or religion

Something special and sacred

Check it out

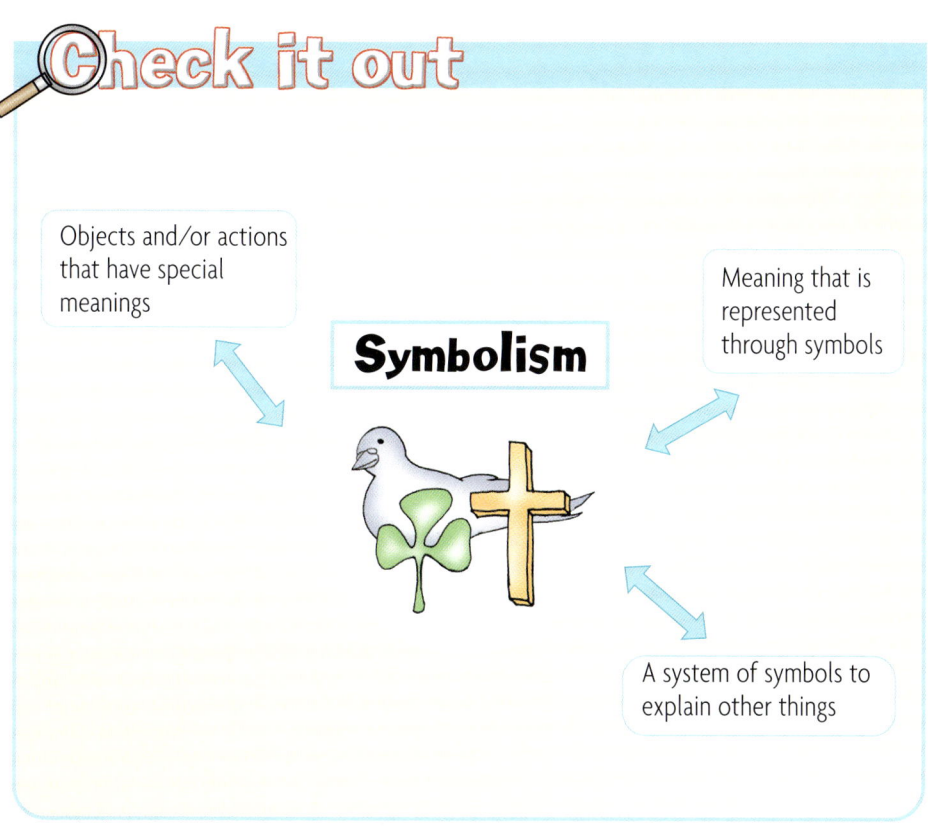

Objects and/or actions that have special meanings

Symbolism

Meaning that is represented through symbols

A system of symbols to explain other things

Within religious traditions, each person will have their own views on what helps them to worship.

'This building has a feeling of holiness; the sacred.'

'I don't need a church to worship my God. The money would be better spent on the poor.'

'We both came here as children; we feel really at home here – it is part of our lives.'

'It's good to meet with others for worship.'

'When we are here together, we are all the same – none better than the other.'

'There is a community spirit here. The music and images help too.'

'It is a duty to attend a place of worship.'

Task

- 'The place doesn't matter; it's who and how you worship!'

Do you agree? Give reasons or evidence for your answer showing that you have thought about more than one point of view.

Write an answer to this evaluative question, using the WAWOS framework. (See page 10)

Exam Tip

It is important when answering questions which ask for a point of view, that you express your thoughts clearly and give reasons for what you think, with either good examples or illustrations, or specific religious teaching to support your view.

Many candidates score low levels of marks because they just state a view without comment, explanation or justification. Also remember that you should *'show that you have thought about more than one point of view.'* So, acknowledge that there are other ideas, which also have reasons and justifications.

 'A place of worship should not have lots of images and symbols; it distracts people from worship.' Do you agree? Give reasons or evidence for your answer showing that you have thought about more than one point of view. [6]

Look at the two answers below. Using the Levels of Response grids on page 1, decide what marks to give to each one. Then, choose one of them, and re-write it so that it gets full marks.

Answer A	Answer B
I do agree. If you are going to a place to worship God, then you should be focused on him and not on other things. Too many places of worship have so many things around, that you start looking at them and thinking about them, and so forget what you came to do. Of course, many, many years ago, it was thought that people who could not read would be helped by having pictures or symbols around the place so they could understand. But there are not many people today who can't read. Anyway, you don't need to be able to read to think and to worship, so I agree with the statement fully.	I do not agree, as the statement does not take account of the reason for the images and symbols. They have actually been put there to help people in their worship. They help to remind worshippers of important things in their faith, or great stories that come from the sacred writings. These can be a stimulus to thinking and to worship. They can also help in the sense that the place of worship is shown to be special, and set aside for worship; and the quietness, the images and symbols, and the rituals being followed all help to stimulate a sense of worship. Some people disagree, and think this is all very distracting. Well they can just go to a different place of worship where there are no symbols and images – no one makes them go; they should choose what's best for them.

An Anglican Church

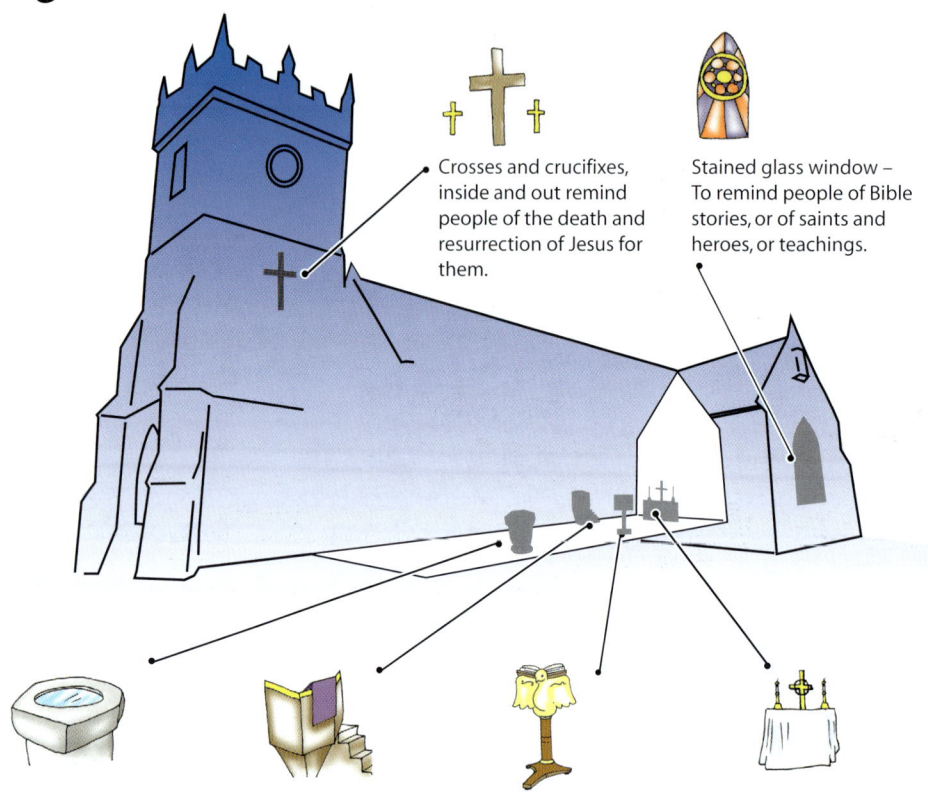

Crosses and crucifixes, inside and out remind people of the death and resurrection of Jesus for them.

Stained glass window – To remind people of Bible stories, or of saints and heroes, or teachings.

Font – Near the front door symbolic of welcoming and entrance to God's family,

Pulpit – For the preaching of the sermon; usually raised to show importance.

Lectern – for reading the Bible and to symbolise the Good News for the world.

Altar – A symbol of God meeting his people, and the place where the bread and wine are consecrated, a symbol of God's sacrifice.

Can you think of other symbols and why they are used?

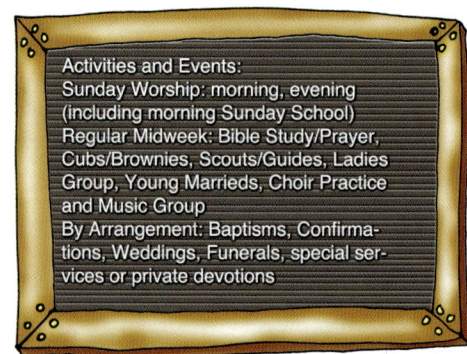

Activities and Events:
Sunday Worship: morning, evening (including morning Sunday School)
Regular Midweek: Bible Study/Prayer, Cubs/Brownies, Scouts/Guides, Ladies Group, Young Marrieds, Choir Practice and Music Group
By Arrangement: Baptisms, Confirmations, Weddings, Funerals, special services or private devotions

Rules of Behaviour

To respect the sacredness of the place and the purposes of those attending for worship by, for example:

- Not talking during the sermon or Bible readings
- Not smoking inside
- Men remove hats or caps on entering
- Avoiding eating in the main sanctuary
- Making sure mobile phones are off!

Some Differences

Some churches will have daily services.

Roman Catholic churches will have a tabernacle, stations of the cross, and confessionals.

Chapels are often simpler, but are likely to have a pulpit, a communion table, and a font or baptistry.

An Orthodox Church

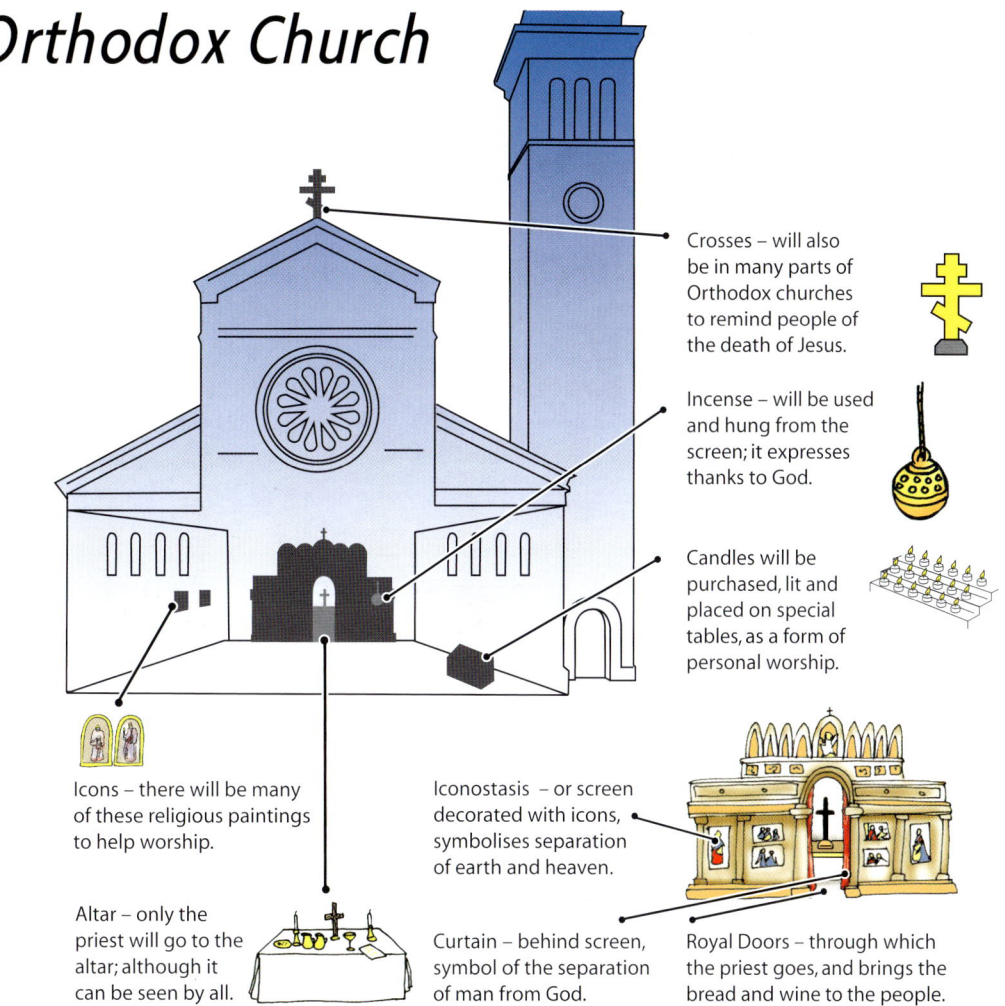

Crosses – will also be in many parts of Orthodox churches to remind people of the death of Jesus.

Incense – will be used and hung from the screen; it expresses thanks to God.

Candles will be purchased, lit and placed on special tables, as a form of personal worship.

Icons – there will be many of these religious paintings to help worship.

Iconostasis – or screen decorated with icons, symbolises separation of earth and heaven.

Altar – only the priest will go to the altar; although it can be seen by all.

Curtain – behind screen, symbol of the separation of man from God.

Royal Doors – through which the priest goes, and brings the bread and wine to the people.

Can you think of other symbols and why they are used?

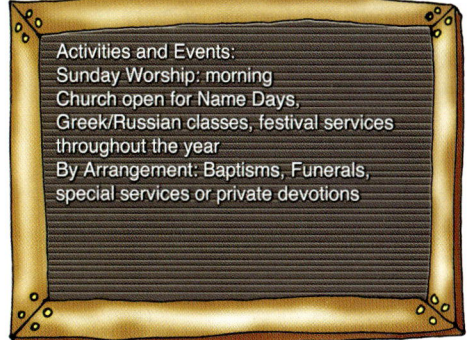

Activities and Events:
Sunday Worship: morning
Church open for Name Days,
Greek/Russian classes, festival services throughout the year
By Arrangement: Baptisms, Funerals, special services or private devotions

Rules of Behaviour

To respect the sacredness of the place and the purposes of those attending for worship by, for example:

- Making the sign of the cross on entry
- Kissing the icons
- Not wearing shorts, and women ensuring their shoulders are covered
- Not smoking inside
- Avoiding eating in the main area of worship
- Making sure mobile phones are off!

A Buddhist Temple
(e.g. Theravada Tradition)

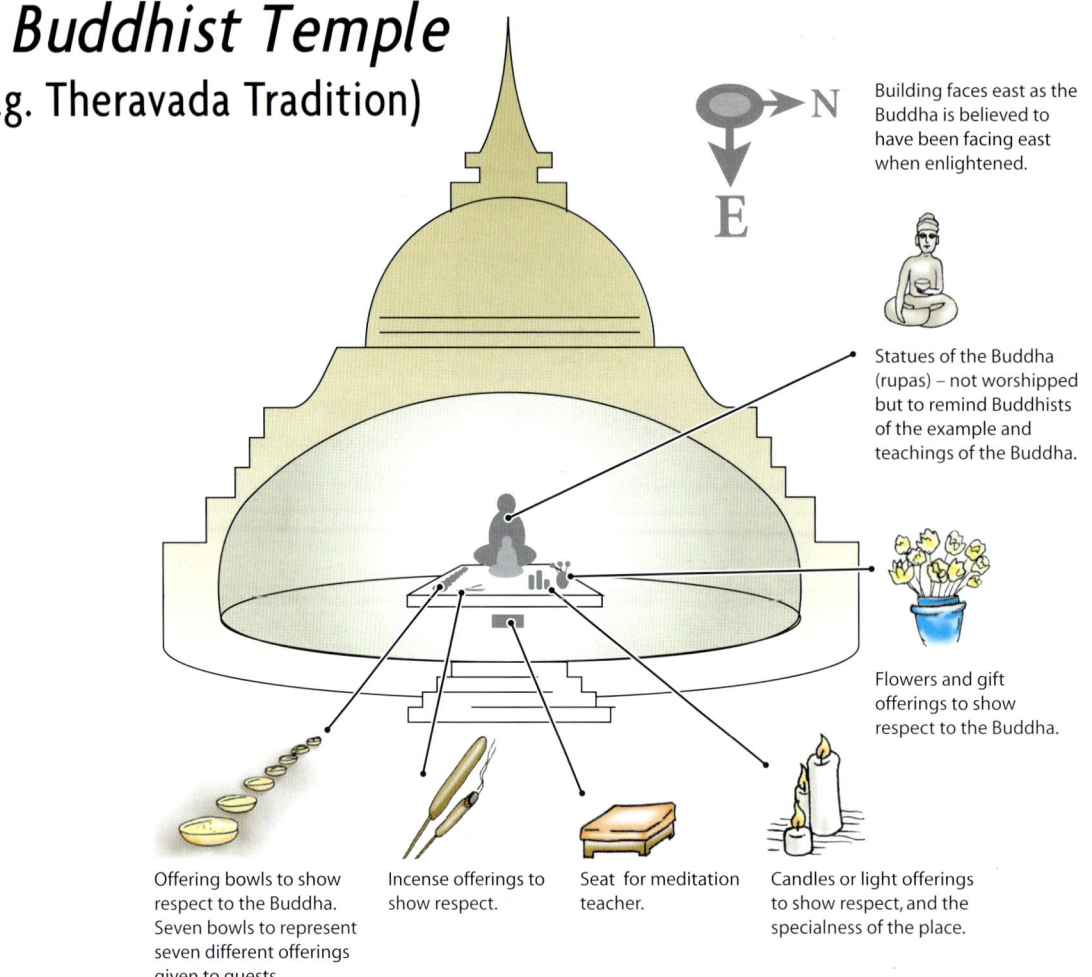

Building faces east as the Buddha is believed to have been facing east when enlightened.

Statues of the Buddha (rupas) – not worshipped but to remind Buddhists of the example and teachings of the Buddha.

Flowers and gift offerings to show respect to the Buddha.

Offering bowls to show respect to the Buddha. Seven bowls to represent seven different offerings given to guests.

Incense offerings to show respect.

Seat for meditation teacher.

Candles or light offerings to show respect, and the specialness of the place.

Can you think of other symbols and why they are used?

Activities and Events:

Days of retreat and meditation

Festival ceremonies throughout the year

Rules of Behaviour

To respect the sacredness of the place and the purposes of those attending by, for example:

- Showing respect to the statue/s of the Buddha:
  - turn to face it
  - often putting hands together
  - and/or bowing
- Taking shoes off
- Not smoking inside
- Avoiding eating in the main shrine
- Making sure mobile phones are off!

Some Differences

Designs of temples differ from country to country, and according to branches of Buddhism. There are many places Buddhists may go to meditate or join in puja. The Mahayanna Buddhists will normally have a central shrine room within the temple campus. Some temple grounds will include a stupa, with a path around it.

A Hindu Mandir

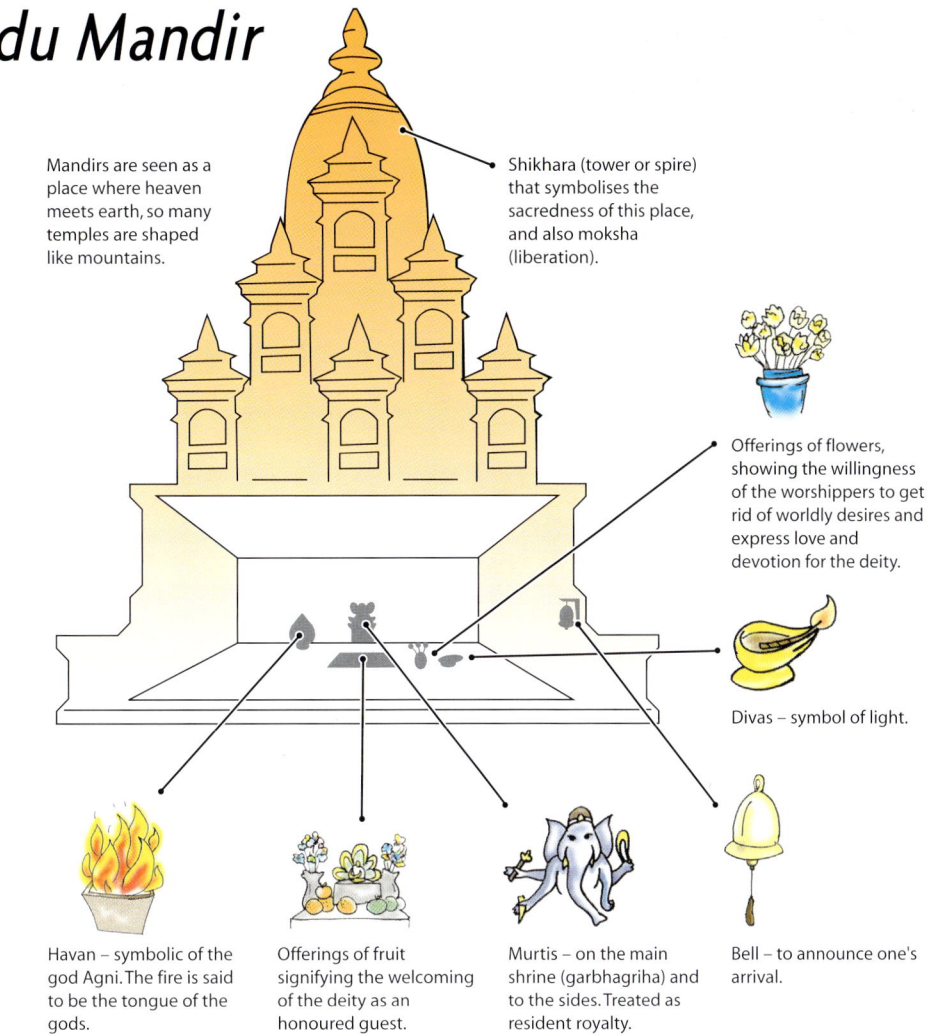

Mandirs are seen as a place where heaven meets earth, so many temples are shaped like mountains.

Shikhara (tower or spire) that symbolises the sacredness of this place, and also moksha (liberation).

Offerings of flowers, showing the willingness of the worshippers to get rid of worldly desires and express love and devotion for the deity.

Divas – symbol of light.

Havan – symbolic of the god Agni. The fire is said to be the tongue of the gods.

Offerings of fruit signifying the welcoming of the deity as an honoured guest.

Murtis – on the main shrine (garbhagriha) and to the sides. Treated as resident royalty.

Bell – to announce one's arrival.

Can you think of other symbols and why they are used?

Activities and Events:

Marriage ceremonies

Sacred Thread ceremonies

Indian dancing and culture schools

Rules of Behaviour

To respect the sacredness of the place and the purposes of those attending for worship by, for example:

- Removing shoes before entering
- Partaking of prashad
- Treating murtis with respect

Some Differences

The arrangement and contents of mandirs differ widely from country to country and in accordance with the tradition within Hinduism to which it belongs.

The home shrine is very important in Hinduism.

A Mosque

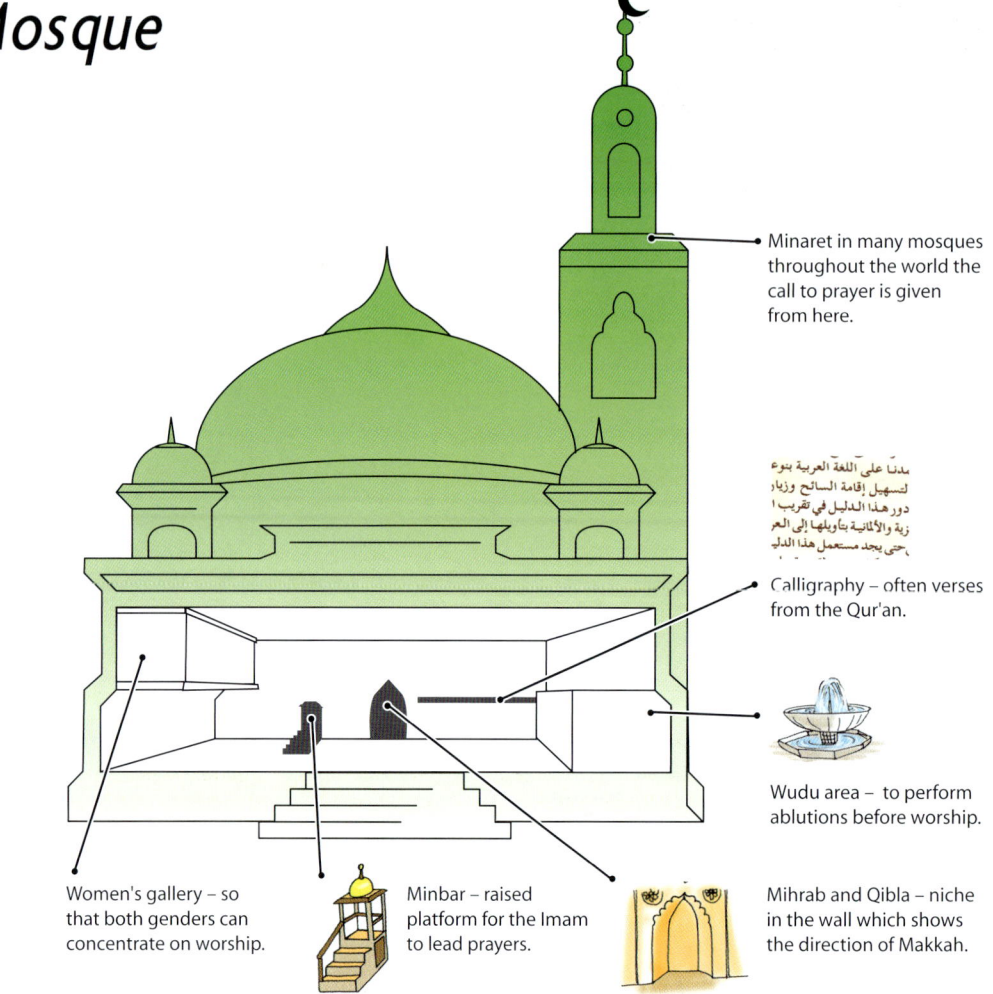

Minaret in many mosques throughout the world the call to prayer is given from here.

مدناً على اللغة العربية بنوء
لتسهيل إقامة الصالح وزياد
دور هذا الدليل في تقريب ا
زية والألمانية بتأويلها إلى العر
حتى يجد مستعمل هذا الدلي

Calligraphy – often verses from the Qur'an.

Wudu area – to perform ablutions before worship.

Women's gallery – so that both genders can concentrate on worship.

Minbar – raised platform for the Imam to lead prayers.

Mihrab and Qibla – niche in the wall which shows the direction of Makkah.

Can you think of other symbols and why they are used?

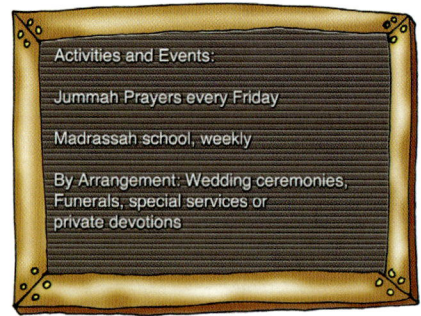

Activities and Events:

Jummah Prayers every Friday

Madrassah school, weekly

By Arrangement: Wedding ceremonies, Funerals, special services or private devotions

Rules of Behaviour

To respect the sacredness of the place and the purposes of those attending for worship by, for example:

- Taking shoes off before entering
- Men and women sitting separately
- Women wearing head covering
- Performing wudu before prayers
- Facing the Kaaba
- Sitting on the floor

A Jewish Synagogue

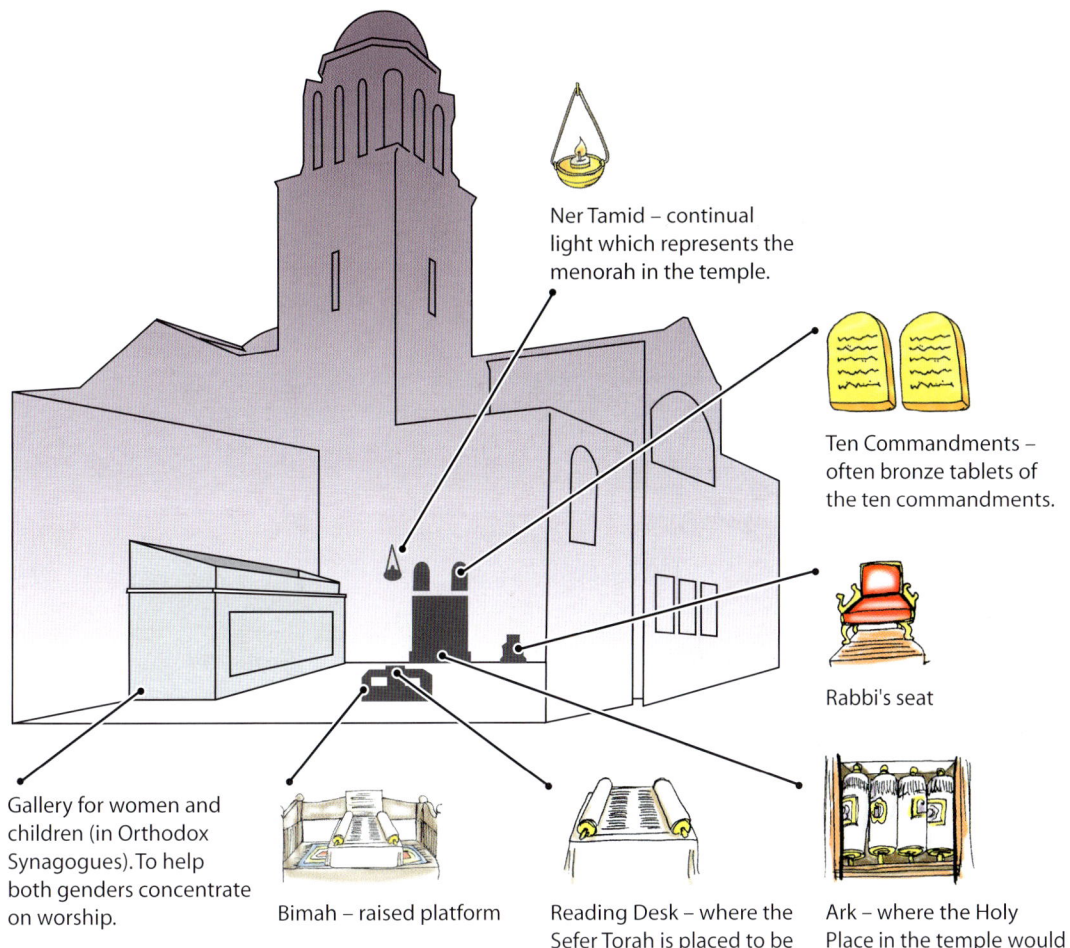

Ner Tamid – continual light which represents the menorah in the temple.

Ten Commandments – often bronze tablets of the ten commandments.

Rabbi's seat

Gallery for women and children (in Orthodox Synagogues). To help both genders concentrate on worship.

Bimah – raised platform

Reading Desk – where the Sefer Torah is placed to be read from.

Ark – where the Holy Place in the temple would have been, where the Sefer Torah is kept.

Can you think of other symbols and why they are used?

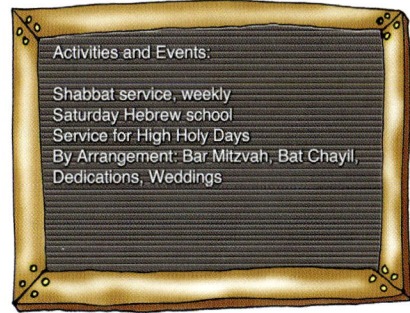

Activities and Events:

Shabbat service, weekly
Saturday Hebrew school
Service for High Holy Days
By Arrangement: Bar Mitzvah, Bat Chayil, Dedications, Weddings

Rules of Behaviour in an Orthodox Synagogue

To respect the sacredness of the place and the purposes of those attending for worship by, for example:

- Men and women sitting separately
- Married women covering their heads
- Men wearing kippot
- Make sure mobile phones are off!

Some Differences

In Reformed Synagogues, men and women sit together.

A Sikh Gurdwara

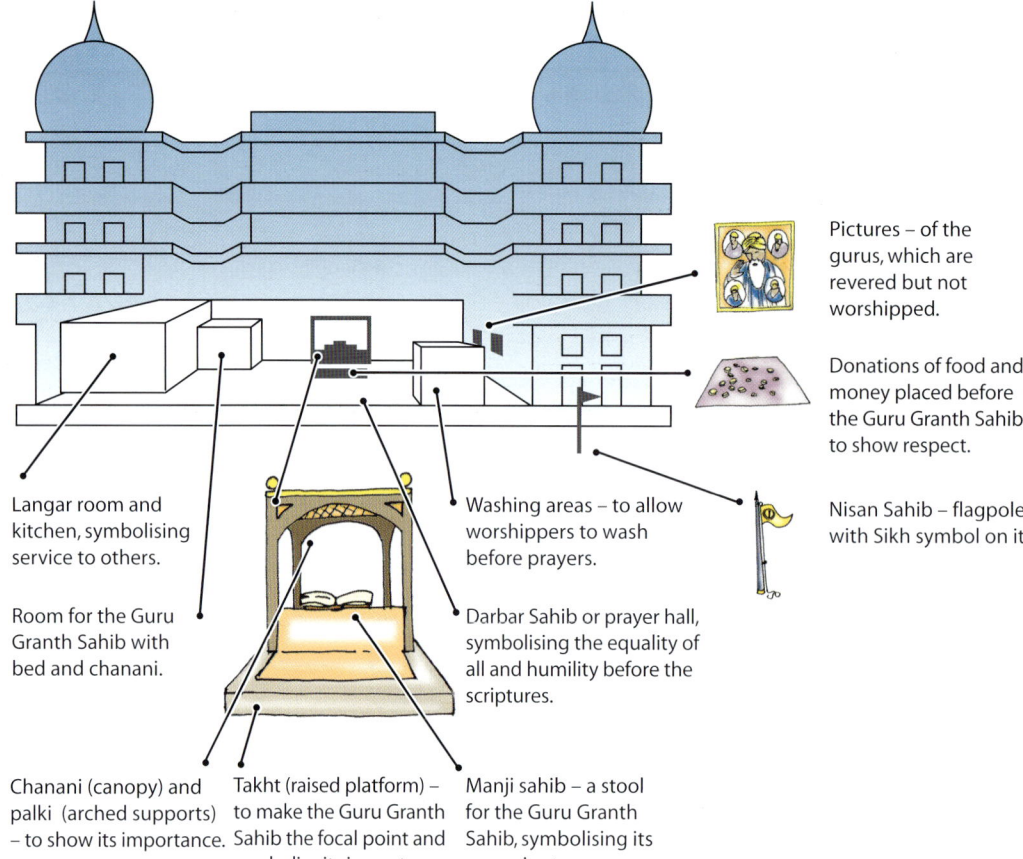

Pictures – of the gurus, which are revered but not worshipped.

Donations of food and money placed before the Guru Granth Sahib to show respect.

Nisan Sahib – flagpole with Sikh symbol on it.

Langar room and kitchen, symbolising service to others.

Room for the Guru Granth Sahib with bed and chanani.

Washing areas – to allow worshippers to wash before prayers.

Darbar Sahib or prayer hall, symbolising the equality of all and humility before the scriptures.

Chanani (canopy) and palki (arched supports) – to show its importance.

Takht (raised platform) – to make the Guru Granth Sahib the focal point and symbolise its importance.

Manji sahib – a stool for the Guru Granth Sahib, symbolising its sovereignty.

Can you think of other symbols and why they are used?

Activities and Events:

Daily Service, Sunday services, Sangrand service, Baisakhi and Divali celebrations, Punjabi classes

By Arrangement: Naming Ceremony, Amrit Ceremony, Weddings, Funerals, Akhand Path service

Rules of Behaviour

To respect the sacredness of the place and the purposes of those attending for worship by, for example:

- Men and women sitting separately
- Covering heads and wearing long skirts or trousers
- Removing shoes
- Kneeling in front of Scriptures and sitting on floor
- Making a donation of food or money
- Receiving karah prashad as leave
- No smoking or alcoholic drinks
- Making sure mobile phones are switched off!

Some Differences

Some gurdwaras do not have pictures of the gurus, as they do not want them to be worshipped or distract from the Guru Granth Sahib

Exam Tip

This unit is all about religious expression, and so it is important to remember that answers to questions about symbols and symbolism in places of worship, will need to refer to **how they are a way of religious expression, or what effect they have on worshippers and their worship**. Always read the question carefully, and look out for key words – do not just write everything you can about a symbol.

Q *Describe how **two** examples of religious symbolism within **one** religious tradition help worshippers express their faith and devotion.*

Look at the answer below. Do you think this answer is worthy of six marks? Explain why. How would you improve it to gain full marks?

Name of religious tradition: Christianity

How symbolism helps worshippers: The bread and wine used in some services reminds people of Jesus' death and sacrifice. It helps them to give thanks to God for what he has done for them. Another kind of symbolism used, are the stained glass windows, with pictures of the stories in the Gospels, or of famous people in Christianity, like Saints or something. They help worshippers to remember stories and to learn from them. This makes them think more deeply about living out their faith.

Task

- Now write a full answer to the same question for the other religion you are studying.

What about other special places?

All religions have places that are special to members of the faith because of their connections in some way with the founder or important leaders, or where some great happening or experience took place. Often, believers make pilgrimages to such places, to show their devotion, or as a witness to their faith, or to grow spiritually through the experience. Some religions require or expect pilgrimage to be made at some time in one's spiritual life. Others have no requirement, but individual believers, or groups from faith communities, do undertake a pilgrimage as part of their spiritual life and experience.

Check it out

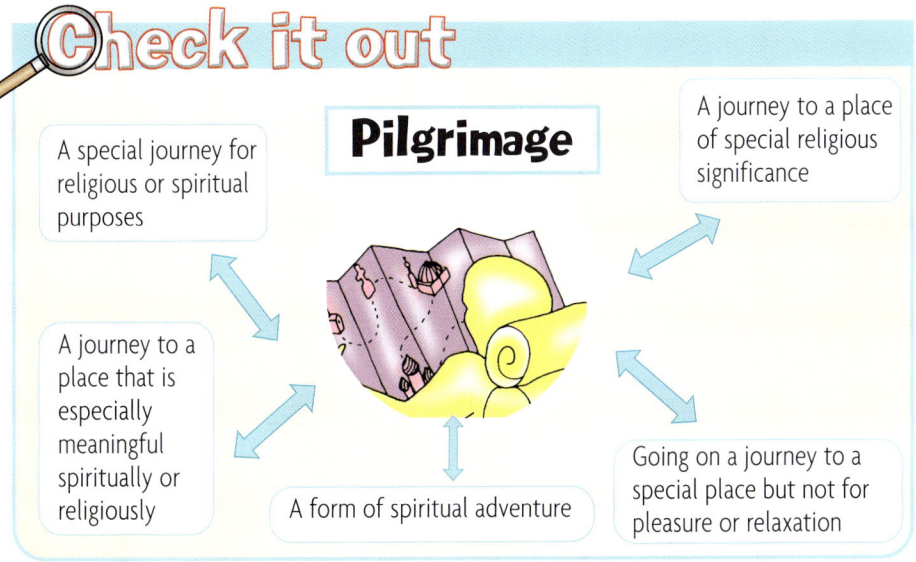

Pilgrimage

A special journey for religious or spiritual purposes

A journey to a place of special religious significance

A journey to a place that is especially meaningful spiritually or religiously

A form of spiritual adventure

Going on a journey to a special place but not for pleasure or relaxation

Christianity ✝

The Holy Land

To walk in the streets where Jesus walked, and to see the places we have so often heard in Bible readings and stories has been absolutely fantastic. The highlight for me was communion in the Garden of Gethsemane. I have never felt anything like it – it was so special. Every communion will be different from now on. Being here and seeing all this and thinking about all that Jesus said and did has made it seem just as if he were here with us. Everyone has felt the same, and some have wept openly as they knelt in prayer. The vicar has been great – I think he has been moved by the way everyone has responded to the visit.

Jonathan

There is no requirement for Christians to go on any pilgrimage, but many Christians wish to visit the Holy Land, and specific sites within it, because of its connections with Jesus and his life.

The Church of the Nativity at Bethlehem, Golgotha (the place where Jesus was crucified) and the Garden tomb in Jerusalem are the most popular sites.

Many pilgrims like to walk along the Via Dolorosa (the path Jesus walked from Pilate to Golgotha), and often will stop and meditate and pray, or listen to the readings of the New Testament about the events.

Find out about another place of Christian pilgrimage.

Look it up
www.toursinisrael.com

Christianity ✝

Lourdes

> I didn't really want to come here because I wasn't sure that it would make any difference to my condition. But it has been truly amazing. Although medically I am no different, I *feel* so different. Stronger somehow, and more able to cope with my illness. And the love that has been shown here, and the sense of God's love is so overwhelming. Isn't it wonderful that so much can happen in a place such as this. Thank you for encouraging me to come!
>
> Molly

One of the most popular Christian pilgrimage sites is Lourdes, in France, where St Bernadette is said to have had a number of visions of the Virgin Mary. There is a spring of water there that is claimed to have healing properties, and many pilgrims go because of illness or disease. Since 1873 there have been about 64 cases declared as miracles, but many people have felt greatly helped by visiting the place because:

- They have felt a real sense of God's presence
- They feel spiritually refreshed and encouraged
- They have a greater sense of community and identity through the experience

Find out about another place of Christian pilgrimage.

Look it up

http://www.re-xs.ucsm.ac.uk/re/pilgrimage

Buddhism ☸

Bodh Gaya and Kapilavastu

To all at Cardiff Road Temple.

Can you see the Bodhi tree? This grew from the seed of the same tree that Buddha sat under when he was meditating. Like the other pilgrims, I walked round the tree and sat under it to meditate. Most of the pilgrims had bare feet and heads, to show their respect. I am so glad I came, it has been really inspiring! I feel that all the meditations and readings we have done back home have suddenly all come together.

Joanna

Buddhists try to make pilgrimages to the principal locations in the life of the Buddha, like Bodh Gaya, where he gained enlightenment, and Kapilavastu, where he was born.

For some Buddhists pilgrimage is believed to:

- Bring about religious merit
- Be inspirational
- Re-affirm religious practices

Find out about another place of Buddhist pilgrimage.

Look it up

http://www.buddhanet.net

Hinduism ॐ

Ganges/Varanasi and Allahabad

Since coming to Varanasi I just feel so different. It is so hard to believe that here I am at the foremost city of Shiva. There are so many reasons why people are here. Some have come in the hope of finding liberation, some to accompany the cremation ghats, and many like to participate in worship at the holy places. Wherever I go there are people taking guidance and listening to talks. I have walked around many temples, and tried to get as near to the Ganges to bathe. So much to think about – so much to do!

Sejal

For Hindus, a special place to die or be cremated is preferred, as this helps give good karma.

Pilgrims travel with a purpose, meditate and reflect.

They hope for spiritual fulfilment. There are about 2000 temples in this region.

Find out about another place of Hindu pilgrimage.

Look it up

http://www.hindunet.org

Islam ☪

Makkah

> Wow! Being here is much more exciting and fantastic than I expected – and I did expect it too! There are thousands of people, but we are all the same – all of one mind and purpose. Wearing the ihram is so special too; I really feel different, and just caught up in all the holiness and spirituality around here. Seeing the Kaaba, and circling it, was quite incredible.
>
> Really looking forward to going to Mina on 10 Dhul Hijja. Tell you all about it when I get back!
>
> Ahmed

For Muslims, the Hajj to Makkah is one of the five duties or pillars expected, provided they are healthy and can manage to pay for the journey.

Special dress for men, called ihram is worn – two unsewn pieces of cloth, one tied round the waist, the other thrown over the shoulder. It is a symbol of holiness and purity, humility and equality, and dedication.

Find out about another place of Muslim pilgrimage.

Look it up
http://www.islam.org/hajj

Judaism

Israel and the Western Wall

I wish you could have come to my Bar Mitzvah in Jerusalem. It was so special going through the ceremony after having been to the Western Wall. I don't think I have ever felt so moved! It has made me really proud to be Jewish, and really determined to live the faith. In a way I suppose that's what Bar Mitzvah is – but I'm so glad we were able to do it here in Israel.

We've taken loads of photographs, and a video of the Bar Mitzvah itself, so you'll see it all when we get back.

Benjamin

According to the Torah all Jews should go to Jerusalem for the three Pilgrim festivals – Passover; Shavuot; Sukkot. After the destruction of the Temple many would go to the ruins of the Western Wall to mourn its destruction. Since the reunification of Israel in 1967 many Jews have considered it important to visit Israel and in particular the Western Wall in Jerusalem and Masada. Many Jews consider it important to visit graves of important spiritual rabbis and scholars.

Find out about another place of Jewish pilgrimage.

Look it up

http://www.virtualjerusalem.com

Sikhism

Amritsar and the Golden Temple

Can't believe I'm here in this great historic city. To think that Guru Nanak once meditated here. Went in to the Golden Temple which was begun to be built by Guru Ram Das in 1573. It is in the middle of a lake, with four doors around it to show people from all parts of the world are welcome. And there are so many people from all over the world! It's so special being here, and realising that this place has been a place of pilgrimage for so long – amidst all the activity, you can just feel the spirituality.

Kanwaljit

Pilgrimage is not a religious duty for Sikhs, but many choose to go for historic reasons to see the places associated with Amritsar and the Golden Temple.

As with other religions, the benefits are seen to be in the increase of spirituality, the demonstration of one's faith to others, and the sense of connection to the past and long standing tradition from which one's religion and its practices come.

Find out about another place of Sikh pilgrimage.

Look it up

http://www.sikhnet.com

Does it matter if the reasons for the place being sacred is true or not?

Sometimes questions are raised about the historical accuracy of events that were supposed to have happened at sacred sites. It must be remembered, however, the purpose of going on pilgrimage is not so much factual or historical, as spiritual.

CASE STUDY

Helen has to complete an evaluation for her RE homework. The question is: *'Going on pilgrimage is a waste of time!' Do you agree? Give reasons or evidence for your answer showing that you have thought about more than one point of view.'* [6]

Helen has thought about what the question means;

She has looked through her notes and books;

She has asked for the views of her family and friends;

These are the points of view she now has to consider:

There is no proof that the actual events happened at these places. How do we know that Jesus was born in Bethlehem?	When you go on pilgrimage you feel a sense of tradition. For centuries Christians have been visiting the Holy Land.	In some religions it is a duty to go on pilgrimage. It is not to be questioned.
Going on pilgrimage is not going on holiday. By visiting the sacred sites people should feel more involved with their religious faith.	You don't have to pay to go on a pilgrimage to show that you are religious.	Going on pilgrimage does not make you a better person.
It doesn't matter if the place being sacred is true or not, it's the participation with other pilgrims that matters.	There are often strong historical links for some places being special to a religious tradition.	Tourism and business commerce are the real profit-makers in places that are supposed to be sacred.
Sometimes the time of the pilgrimage is as important as the place (because of a special anniversary).	**Can you add any more views or ideas yourself?**	

Helen now has to decide which of the comments are for and against the argument, and decide which four arguments she thinks are best, and that she can give extra details to.

Which four points would you choose, and what extra information would you give to each?

- Now complete the evaluation question, using the WAWOS framework. (See page 10)

Mission and evangelism

Within some religions, there is an expectation or an emphasis on making an effort to tell other people about the faith. This may take many forms, such as giving out pamphlets (often called 'tracts'), holding special 'evangelistic' services or missions, making door-to-door visits in a particular neighbourhood, or simply individuals telling their friends and neighbours about their beliefs, and inviting them to join them at events in their place of worship.

Mission

Mission is a word that means 'the act of sending', or, 'the duty on which a person is sent'. So in religion it referred to the act of going out to preach the faith to others – because the person (or missionary) was sent.

Evangelism

'Evangel' is a word meaning 'good tidings' or 'the Gospel'. So evangelism has come to mean the ways and means some religions take to spread their beliefs to others. A person engaged in this sort of work would be called 'an evangelist'.

Conversion

This is a term meaning a change from one religion to another, or from no religion to being a religious person.

Within some religious traditions, attitudes to mission and evangelism vary greatly. Some branches of Christianity – those sometimes referred to as 'evangelical' or 'evangelistic' – feel that telling others about the faith, so as to lead to 'conversion' is an important task and duty of the Christian. They believe it is what Jesus commissioned them to do. Others feel that it is right and proper to be open about one's faith, and even to share it with others, but that people need to make their own personal choices about what to believe.

As far as most other religions are concerned, there is always a willingness to share faith with others, and a willingness to accept those who do convert to the religion from elsewhere, but there is less emphasis on mission and evangelism as described above.

Sharing one's faith

Whenever people believe in something, and it is important to them and their way of life, they inevitably like to talk about it with others. Sometimes this will be with others who share the same beliefs, or it may be to tell others who don't share that belief, as described above. Many people share their faith with others in order to promote a mutual understanding.

Check it out

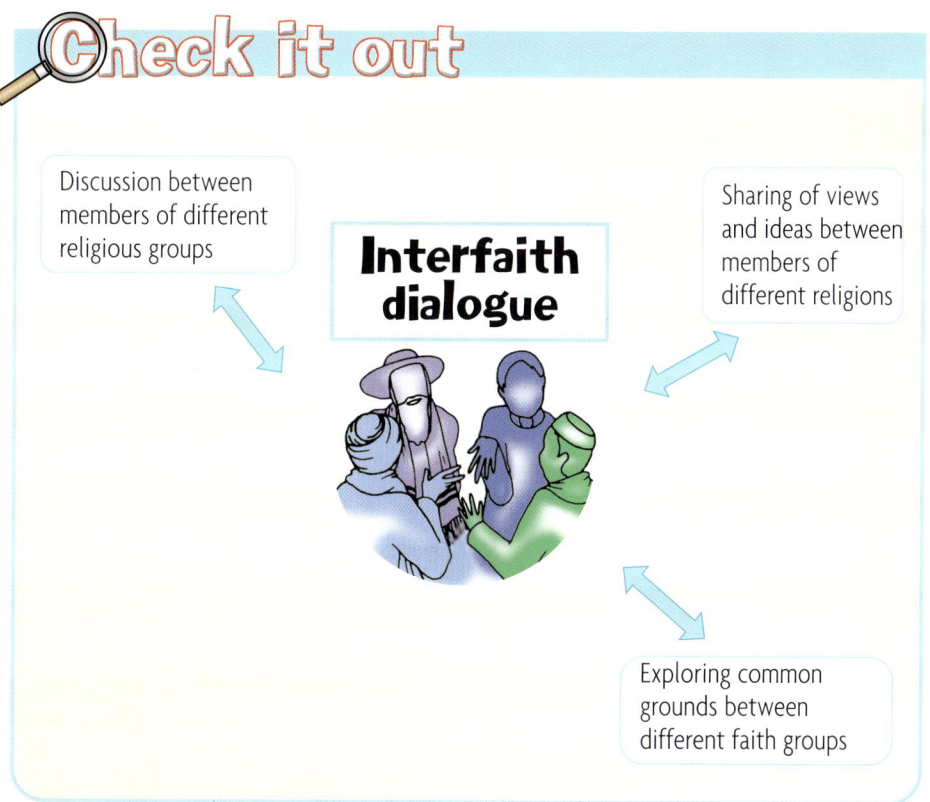

Discussion between members of different religious groups

Sharing of views and ideas between members of different religions

Interfaith dialogue

Exploring common grounds between different faith groups

Interfaith
Activity Group

Collective worship in schools

Working together after disaster or tragedy

Prison visiting

Prayer worship room – e.g. airports

When is sharing one's faith:

Raising awareness	**?**
Creating harmony	
Unacceptable intrusion	

Street Evangelists

Council of Faiths in cities

Corrymeela

Evangelistic crusade

Literature Tracts

Task

- Select one image for each of the following which you think:
  - helps to raise awareness
  - creates harmony
  - is an unacceptable intrusion.

Explain your choices, giving reasons for your answer, and show that you recognise that others may think differently.

The Importance of Interfaith Dialogue in Religious Traditions

As mentioned in the previous section on mission and evangelism, there are differing attitudes within religious traditions as to interfaith dialogue.

On this 'wall' are examples of quotes from individuals within the traditions expressing their view about the matter.

'No peace among the nations without peace among the religions; no peace among the religions without dialogue between the religions.'

Hans Kung

Sikism

'The founder of our religion, Guru Nanak, said in his very first sermon that "There is neither Hindu nor Muslim." What he meant by that was not that Hindus and Muslims, or for that matter Sikhs, Christians, Jews and other faiths, do not exist. Rather, he meant that God does not look at religious labels but at how we live and how we act. To follow on from that teaching, Guru Arjan, the fifth Guru, in compiling the Guru Granth Sahib also included verses by Hindus and Muslims in our holy books in order to show respect of other religions. He also asked a Muslim holy man to lay the foundation stone of the Golden Temple to show this respect for other religions. Then the ninth Guru, Guru Tegh Bahadur, gave his life defending the right of those of another religion to worship in the manner of their choice.'

Indarjit Singh

Buddhism

'I have for many years now engaged in interfaith dialogue and understanding with the basic belief that many major religions of the world have the same potential to transform people into better human beings. The common messages of love, kindness, tolerance, self-discipline and a sense of sharing are in some ways the foundation for respecting the fundamental and basic human rights of every person. The world religions therefore contribute to peace, harmony and human dignity.'

Dalai Lama

Christianity

'There are Christians who see 'dialogue' as a way to convert others. They point to Jesus saying, 'No one comes to the Father except through me' (John14:6). Others hope that dialogue will create a new unified understanding of God, as the reality that underlies all religions. St Paul understood human distinctions of religion, culture and status dissolving when people are united in God, but he saw those divisions overcome by being on in Christ.'

(Gal 3:28, Col 3:11)

'Other Christians see dialogue as a way of promoting peace and justice, through understanding and mutual respect. They point to Jesus' debate with a foreign woman (Mark 7:24–30), and his use of the Samaritan as a caring neighbour (Luke 10: 25–37), as examples of being open to others. This approach expects both partners in the dialogue to contribute something, to learn from each other, and to be changed by the process.
It is perhaps interesting that some Christians hold more than one of these views together.'

Rev Simon Walkling, United Reformed Church Minister, North Wales

The Importance of Interfaith Dialogue in Religious Traditions

Islam	Hinduism	Judaism
'People need to learn more about their neighbours so that ignorance doesn't breed more fanaticism.' Yusuf Islam	'God's grace is like a strong wind that's always blowing. But we have to raise our own sails.' Ramakrishna (1834–1886) A Brahmin who believed that God is present in every religion.	'One of the greatest achievements of the second half of the twentieth century is that this previously troubled relationship (between faiths), the cause of so much pain and suffering has begun to be healed, and in the process new hope has been given to humanity.' Dr Jonathan Sacks, Chief Rabbi of Great Britain and the Commonwealth.

Look it up

www.uri.org.uk (United Religions Initiative)

www.interfaith.org.uk (Inter-Faith Network for the UK)

Task

- Take the two quotes from the religions you are studying, and try to explain in your own words what the person is actually saying. Construct from them a list of points about interfaith dialogue that you can remember for the examination.

TEST IT OUT

(a) Why might believers want to go to a place of worship? [2]

(b) What does *holy* mean? [2]

(c) Explain **two** reasons why some believers go to a place of pilgrimage. [4]

(d) Explain why the Holy Land is an important place of pilgrimage for many Christians. [4]

(e) Describe from **two** different religious traditions how believers might share their faith with others. [6]

(f) 'It doesn't matter how you treat a place of worship – it's only a building after all'. Do you agree? Give reasons or evidence for your answer, showing that you have thought about more than one point of view. [6]

4 Authority – Religion and State

The Big Picture

Why should we obey the law?

Why do people keep the laws?

How do we treat someone who breaks the law?

How should we deal with offenders?

What if the law is wrong?

Questions to think about

Words to know, understand and use: ▼

LAW	
	COMMUNITY
DUTY	
	CONSCIENCE
HUMAN RIGHTS	
	JUSTICE

Religious teachings to explore:

- The role of sacred texts as a source of authority
- Attitudes to crime and justice
- Attitudes to capital punishment
- The relationship between religion and society
- The importance of an individual action to support human rights

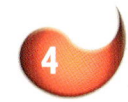

Why should we obey the law?

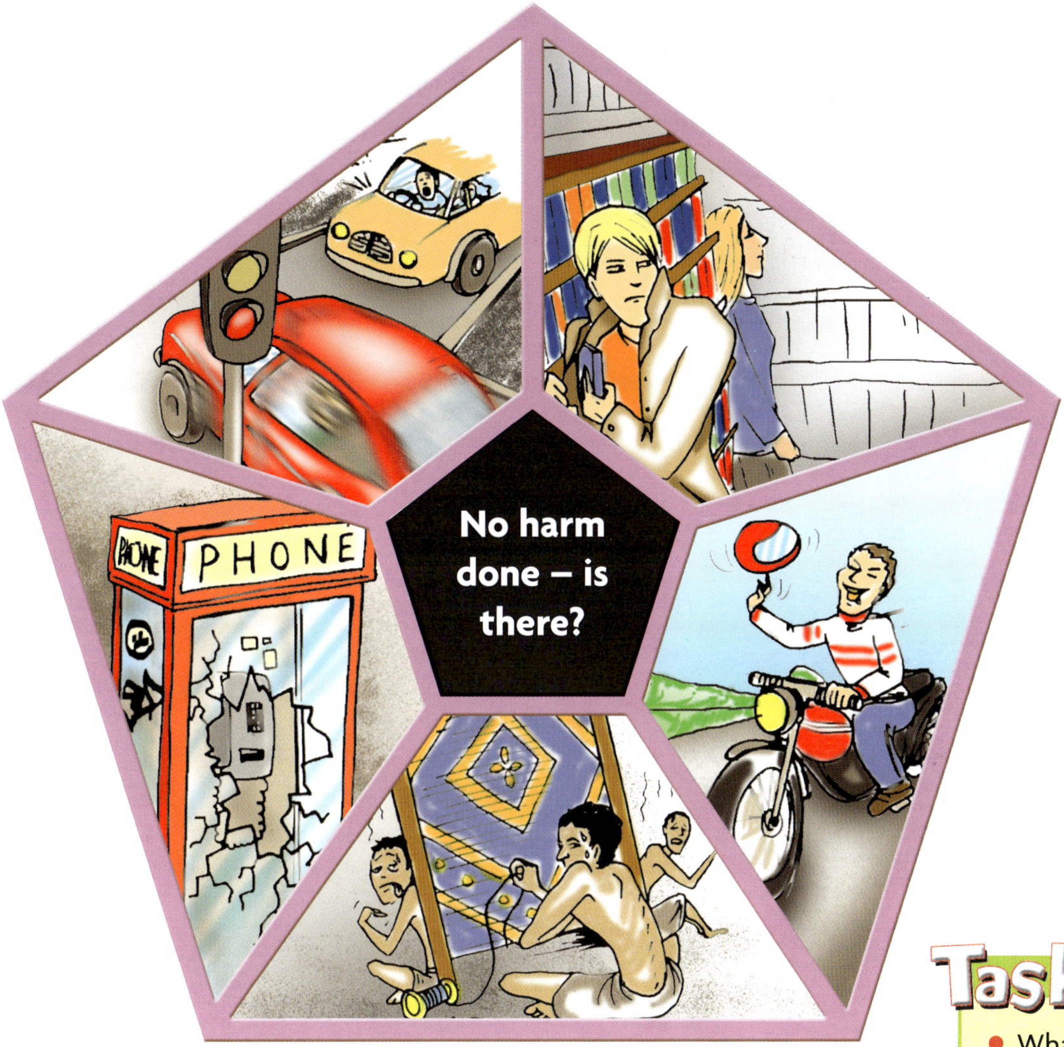

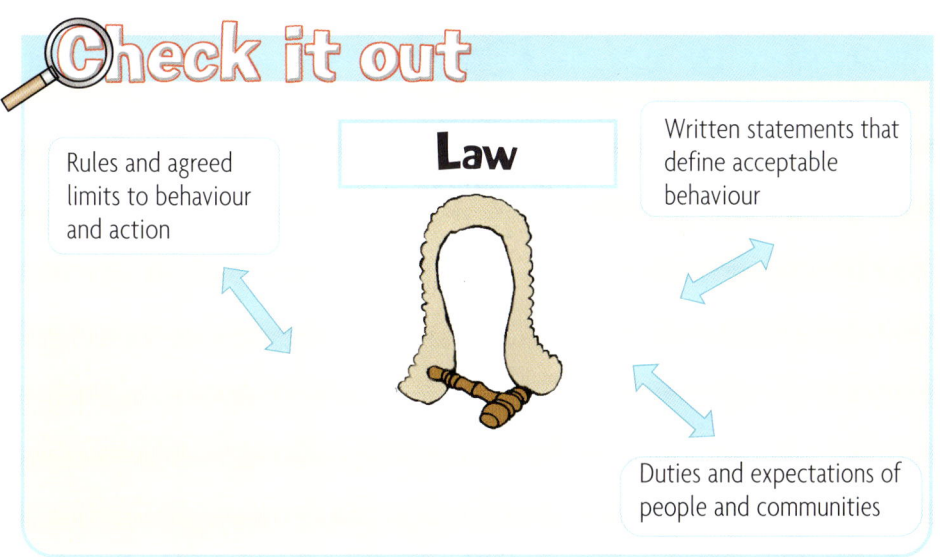

No harm done – is there?
PHONE
PHONE

Task

- What laws are being broken?
- What are the consequences?
- Why do we need laws?

Check it out

Law

Rules and agreed limits to behaviour and action

Written statements that define acceptable behaviour

Duties and expectations of people and communities

Laws are made by the Government, in the Houses of Parliament, and are enforced by the Police and the Law Courts.

Some laws are made by local Councils, and these are also be enforced by the Police and the courts.

The Houses of Parliament, Westminster

Rules, on the other hand, are agreements about how something is done, or the actions that are allowed in a certain place or activity. For example, there are rules about sporting games, like football and hockey – so that everyone knows what can and cannot be done. There are also rules about belonging to a certain club, or using a particular place (such as a library), or a piece of equipment (such as a hired machine).

Breaking laws and rules usually result in some sort of penalty. If a person breaks a law, then they may go to a court and be charged with an offence, and after trial be punished with a prison sentence, a fine, or some community service. For some laws, such as parking or speeding offences, there is no court action, just a fine, and points on a driving licence.

Breaking laws and rules may also lead to some form of penalty – perhaps a fine, or being sent from the game or club, or being banned completely.

Why do people keep laws?

'I don't want to get punished!'

'It's against my conscience to break the laws.'

'It's your duty to the community to obey the laws.'

'Society needs to be safeguarded.'

'Those who are weak need to be protected.'

'Everyone is entitled to their basic human rights.'

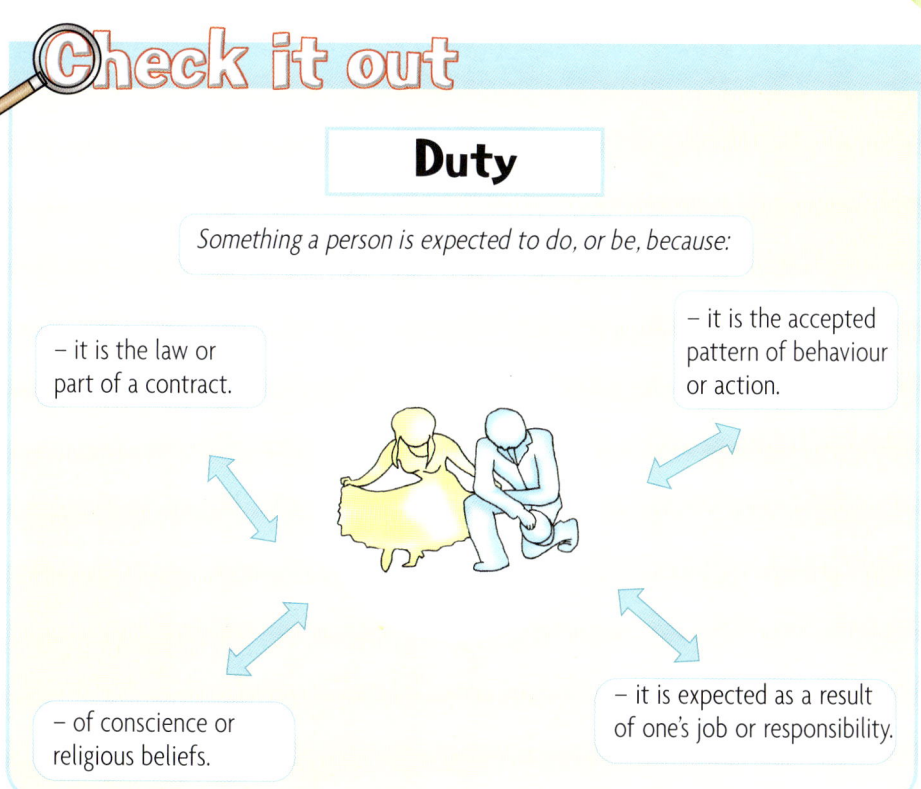

Check it out

Duty

Something a person is expected to do, or be, because:

– it is the law or part of a contract.

– it is the accepted pattern of behaviour or action.

– of conscience or religious beliefs.

– it is expected as a result of one's job or responsibility.

Check it out

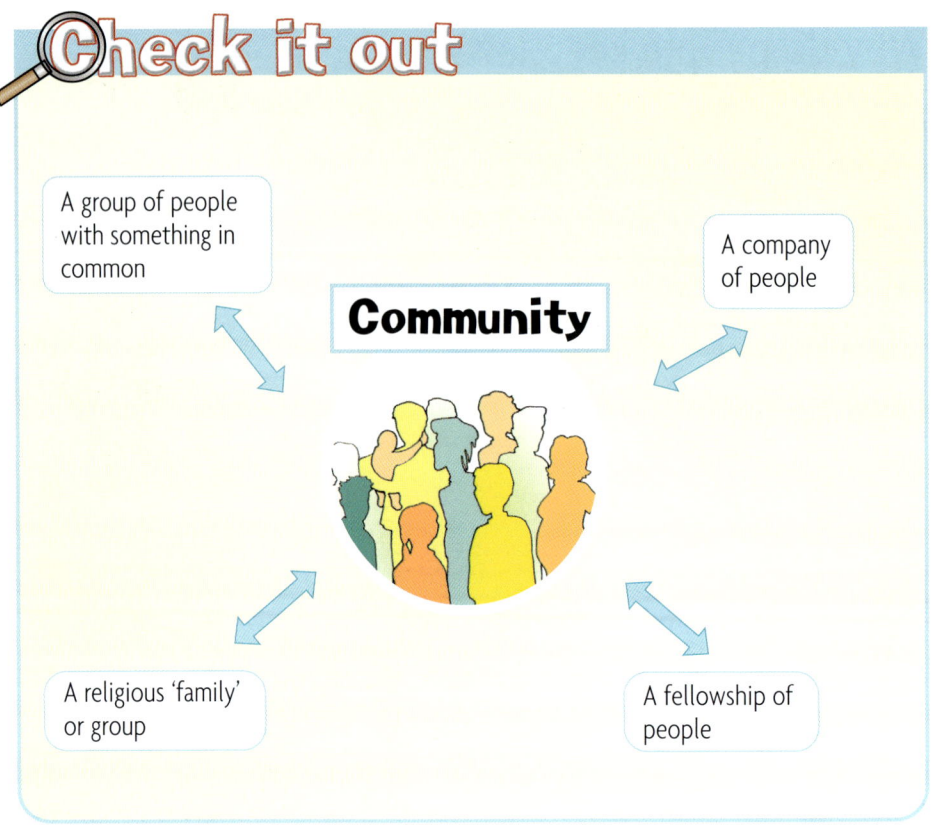

Community

A group of people with something in common

A company of people

A religious 'family' or group

A fellowship of people

Check it out

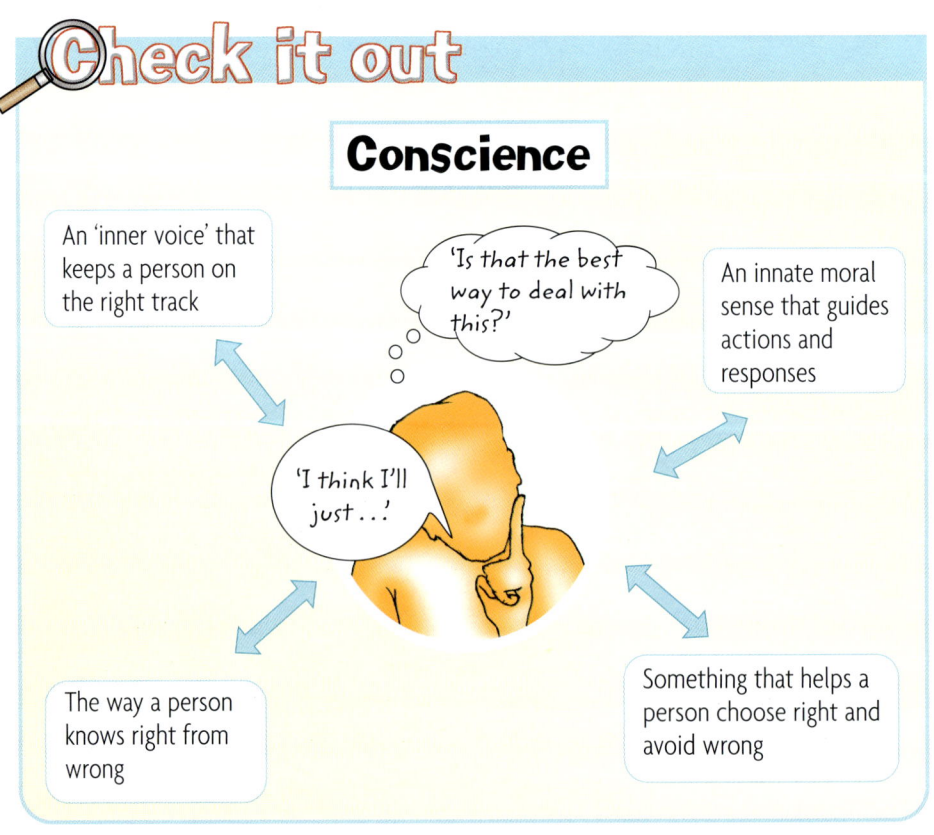

Conscience

An 'inner voice' that keeps a person on the right track

'Is that the best way to deal with this?'

'I think I'll just...'

An innate moral sense that guides actions and responses

The way a person knows right from wrong

Something that helps a person choose right and avoid wrong

Exam Tip

Remember to give accurate descriptions, explanations and spellings of key words and concepts. There is a list in the specification, which you need to learn. There are many other words which you would be expected to know and use correctly – your teacher will have probably given you a list. Learn these too!

 What is 'conscience'? [2]

Look at the three answers below. One was given no marks, one was given one mark and the other two marks. Can you work out which was which, and why?

Answer A	Answer B	Answer C
It is what is in your mind, and is something you have from birth.	Conscience is an innate ability in human beings that enables them to judge what is right and what is wrong. So it guides them in their living.	Conscience is knowing right and wrong.

Task

- A useful idea is to compile a list of important words, with their meanings and contexts. If you haven't already started to do so, begin collecting and completing that list now.

- It would be worth having a list for each of the units in this course. Putting them on postcards will allow you to keep them with you, and remind yourself – and others – of the words and meanings. It is a great way to revise and keep up with learning them.

How do we treat people who break the laws?

Retribution	**Reparation**	**Reform**
A form of revenge on behalf of those who were wronged or subject to attack.	Criminals should have the right to 'pay' for the wrong they have done – to show they are sorry and 'repair' the damage done.	Trying to ensure the criminal is helped to change their approach and way of life.

Aims of Punishment

Protection	**Vindication**	**Deterrence**
Making sure that all people, and society itself, is kept free from possible recurring of a crime by a criminal; criminals themselves also need protection.	To show that the law and authority are of supreme importance; and ensure that the law is upheld, and justified.	To try and deter (or discourage) people from committing crimes at all, because they know what the punishment is, and know it will be given to those caught committing a crime.

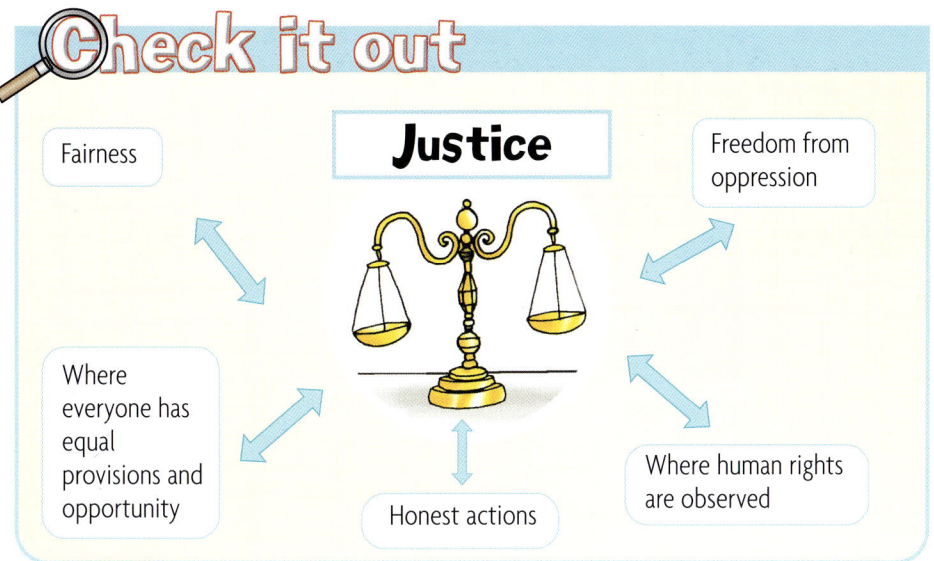

Check it out

Fairness

Justice

Freedom from oppression

Where everyone has equal provisions and opportunity

Honest actions

Where human rights are observed

What about religious laws?

When people belong to a religious community they also have sacred laws (or duties) which they follow. These often come from sacred or holy books of teachings that the whole community is expected to follow. They are seen as of a high status, as they are believed to either come from God directly, or through his inspiration, or because they have deep roots in the history and tradition of the faith.

That means that they are not options to follow, but have a deeper basis, which puts a stronger requirement or sense of duty and responsibility on the part of the believer. For this reason, these act as an authority which people will often consult for guidance, for inspiration, for challenge, and for comfort. Many people will consult their sacred texts when they are facing an issue or dilemma.

'It is the Word of God.'

'It contains stories that show the importance of my faith.'

Holy Books

'It contains guidance on how to live and behave.'

CHRISTIANITY ✝

B **ible** is the name given to the Christian Scriptures. It is made up of two parts, the Old and the New Testaments. Altogether there are 66 different books in the Bible (written in Hebrew and Greek), covering many centuries of life and faith. The Bible has a special place in worship, and many Christians read from it every day.

I **nspired** by God. For some Christians this means it is literally 'the Word of God'; for others, it is believed that God speaks through the Bible, by inspiring Christians as they read and consider its insights and the timeless stories and messages that were written by people inspired by God.

B **asis of faith** – the Bible is the source book of the Christian faith, and it is, particularly in Protestant Churches, seen as the supreme authority in matters of doctrine and belief. This means that it needs to be read, studied and interpreted, by individuals and communities.

L **iving Word** – is the term used by Christians to describe Jesus. They believe him to be 'God made Flesh', and so the clearest way through which God and his will and purpose can be known. This is why the Gospels are so important; they tell of the life and teachings of Jesus, and were written to inspire faith in him.

E **ssential reading**. That is why the Bible has been translated into many different languages, as Christians believe people should read it for themselves and be inspired by it, and try to live according to its teachings and examples.

How do Christians treat people who break the laws?

'Repay no one evil for evil, but take thought for what is noble in the sight of all. If possible, so far as it depends upon you, live peaceably with all. Beloved, never avenge yourselves, but leave it to the wrath of God; for it is written, "Vengeance is mine, I will repay, says the Lord." No, "if your enemy is hungry, feed him; if he is thirsty, give him a drink; for by so doing you will heap burning coals upon his head." Do not be overcome by evil, but overcome evil with good.'

Romans 12: 17–21

Christians would turn to the Bible for support and guidance. One passage that would be important for this issue would be:

Christianity is a religion of forgiveness. It teaches that by following the examples of Jesus people are forgiven by God, and so believers should act in a similar manner and forgive others.

This does not mean liking the person. When Pope John Paul II survived an assassination, he asked for mercy for the person who had tried to kill him.

However, some Christians would also argue that although it is good to forgive someone for a wrong they have done, and give them a new start, there is also the idea of justice, and that means that there should be a punishment. They would say that punishment and forgiveness can – and should – go together.

The Bible

The Pali Canon

BUDDHISM

P　**ali Canon** is the collection of the teachings of the Buddha. It was written down in the language of Pali about 500 years after the life of the Buddha and is mostly used by Theravada Buddhists.

A　**nother name** for the Pali Canon is the Tripitaka or Three Baskets – the Vinaya Pitaka, Sutta Pitaka, and Abhidamma Pitaka.

L　**aws** or rules that monks and nuns should follow are in the first basket (Vinya Pitaka). There is also a section which contains the laws of the Sangha as well as for individual monks. These are kept by the community of monks who recite the 227 rules fortnightly.

I　**mportant teachings** of the Buddha are found in the second basket (Sutta Pitaka). This also contains the Dhammapada containing the Four Noble Truths and the Noble Eightfold Path. The teachings on meditation are followed by most Buddhists today. The Dhammapada is most likely to be found in a Buddhist's home.

C　**hildren enjoy** the Jataka stories found in the Sutta. The stories contain teachings about moral behaviour.

A　**bhidhamma Pitaka** is the third basket, and this is a philosophical commentary on the teachings of the Buddha. It is normally only read by the educated monk and the teachings passed on.

N　**oble Eightfold Path** is contained in the Sutta Pitaka. These are the eight ways people should live by in order to reach enlightenment.

O　**bserving the teachings** of the Pali Canon is essential for all Buddhists. The Buddha insisted that it was his message that was important – not him as a person. Parts of the Canon are often buried in stupas.

N　**uns and monks** will recite selections in the monastery at morning and evening prayers.

How do Buddhists treat people who break the laws?

In Buddhism the root of evil is ignorance and delusion. A sinful or wrong act (pap) produces bad karma which might result in rebirth in the hell states.

Buddhist countries do have a system of punishment as there is a fear that there would be more violence without a system. Many Buddhists disagree with the concept of retribution as they say this is opposed to the teaching of metta (loving kindness) and karuna (compassion). This is particularly the argument against capital punishment, although some Buddhists argue for alternatives that are non-violent.

'As sweet as honey is an evil deed, so thinks the fool so long as it ripens not; but when it ripens, then he comes to grief.'

Dhammapada 69, 71

HINDUISM ॐ

There are many Hindu authoritative texts. One of the best known is The Song of the Lord, or Bhagavad Gita.

ita or Bhagavad Gita is also known as 'The Song of the Lord', and forms part of the Mahabharata.

nspirational. It is a much loved book and many Hindus can recite at least a part of it. It is told in story form and in plays and films. Gandhi kept a copy of it with him at all times. It is often used for personal study and group recitation. Verses are often recited at a funeral.

reated with respect. It is not placed on the floor nor touched with the feet or dirty hands. Copies are sometimes wrapped in silk cloth.

rjuna's conversation with Krishna is a particularly important teaching text. In his conversation, Krishna advises Arjuna that although he may live or die, the outcome is in the hands of God. He should focus on truth and justice. Many Hindus will consult the dialogue for teachings on varnashramadharma (the rules and laws which govern the duties of one's particular caste and stage of life.)

How do Hindus treat people who break the laws?

'Perform your prescribed duty, which is better than not working. Whoever does not work will not succeed even in keeping his body in good repair.'

Bhagavad Gita 3:8

Any form of sin is an act against dharma (duty). For the Hindu their dharma includes self-control, religious and social duty, rules and customs in religious ceremonies and worship, good conduct, and their keeping to the law.

The rules for varnashramadharma are contained in the holy texts and there are punishments or danda. This includes retribution, restraint and reformation.

The Gita

The Qur'an

ISLAM ☪

**ur'an** is the collection of messages revealed by Allah to the Prophet Muhammad over a period of 23 years. Muslims believe that the Qur'an is speaking the word of Allah. .

ltimate guidance for Muslim life. It covers all aspects for all times – unchanging. The message and rules in the Qur'an are for all time. For this reason the Qur'an should be read in Arabic (as it was revealed). Many Muslims become hafiz (learn the Qur'an off by heart).

espect is shown by the way the Qur'an is treated. When not in use it should be stored on a high shelf and wrapped in cloth. Before handling it a person should be in a state of wudu and in a suitable frame of mind. When it is being read it will often be placed on a wooden stand.

khlaq (person's attitudes, conduct and ethics) are described in the Qur'an. The Islamic law (shariah) comes from the Qur'an and Sunnah as it details whether actions in life are halal or haram and how to live the way that Allah wishes.

ations which have become Islamic States have adopted the shariah law as the law of the country.

How do Muslims treat people who break the laws?

Within Islam forgiveness and reconciliation are very important but so also is the need to protect the whole of society.

Punishment is seen as an integral aspect of justice to stop people straying from what is good and just.

For many Muslims there are two acts which deserve capital punishment.
- Murder
- Openly attacking and threatening the Muslim way of life, having previously belonged to Islam

'The good deed and the evil deed cannot be equal. Repel the evil deed with one which is better, then he who was your enemy will become like a close friend.'

Surah 41:34

'The reward for an injury is an equal injury in return, but whoever forgives and makes reconciliation, his reward is due from Allah.'

Surah 42:40

JUDAISM

T

enakh is also known as the Written Torah. It consists of the five books of the Law (Torah), the books of the Prophets (Neviim) and the holy writings (Ketuvim). The word 'Tenakh' is made up from the first letters of each of the three words.

E

ternal. The Tenakh is considered as the message for all time as it contains the Torah which is believed to be the Word of God, and contains rules about how Jews should lead their lives. In addition to the Tenakh, the Talmud is also considered very important by many Jews. This contains the Mishnah, or Oral Torah, which are additional teachings given to Moses by God.

N

eviim is the second part of the Tenakh, and contains stories of the Prophets who were messengers sent to earth by God to teach people, e.g. Isaiah, Amos.

A

uthority. The Tenakh is used as a source of authority throughout Jewish worship, festivals and daily life. The Sefer Torah in the synagogue is treated with great respect. It is placed in the ark in the Synagogue, and a yad used to read it. If the scroll is damaged, it must not be thrown away but buried with as much respect as if it were a person.

K

etuvim are the third section of the Tenakh, and although considered holy, they are not seen to be as sacred as the Torah. They contain writings such as Psalms, which may be used in worship, and the stories of Esther and Ruth, which are read at the festivals of Purim and Shavuot.

H

alakah. This is the collective name referring to the whole of Jewish law as well as to individual laws. It has been built up over the centuries by rabbis to suit modern day issues, e.g. 'Can Jews receive transplant organs from pigs?'. From their considerations, a Responsa is issued.

How do Jews treat people who break laws?

'You shall love your neighbour as yourself.'

Deuteronomy 17: 6

'Anyone who commits murder shall be put to death... The principle is a life for a life.'

Leviticus 24: 17–18

The Torah and Talmud contain many laws giving instruction and guidance about behaviour as well as how crime should be punished.

As Jews believe everyone was given freewill people must take responsibility for their actions. Jews see that the aims of punishment include deterrence, protection, retribution and promoting justice. Justice is very important in Judaism. As God created a just world so Jews must practice justice themselves. Deuteronomy 16 states that judges must be appointed who are fair and do not accept bribes.

At Yom Kippur many Jews repent wrongful actions. One of the statements in the Yom Kippur service is 'Repentance, Charity and Devotion can change a grim fate.' Although Jews are taught they should be forgiving, only the victim can forgive. No one can be forgiven on behalf of others.

SIKHISM ☬

G

uru Granth Sahib are the Sikh Scriptures – sometimes known as Adi Granth.

U

ltimate guide for all Sikhs. After the death of Guru Gobind Singh there were to be no more human gurus, instead all Sikhs would be led by this holy book.

R

espect is shown by the way it is treated in the gurdwara. It is not worshipped. When not being read in the gurdwara, it will be covered with three pieces of embroidered cloth, known as rumala.

U

niform. All are written the same in the Gurmukhim script, with 1,430 pages and 3,384 hymns.

G

urdwaras have the Guru Granth as the place of focus, and there is also a special room where it is 'put to bed' at night.

R

ead by the Granthi, and whilst it is being read a chauri (made of yak's hair fastened to a handle of wood or metal) is waved over the Guru Granth. It is a symbol of authority and power – a reminder to treat the Guru Granth in the same way as royalty.

A

khand paths are continuous or uninterrupted readings of the scriptures, usually used to observe a gurpurb, or festival of the anniversary of a Guru's birthday or death.

N

aming ceremony. The Guru Granth is used in the naming ceremony of babies. At a point in the ceremony, the granthi opens the holy book at random, and reads out the first word on the left-hand page. The parents then choose a name for their baby beginning with the first letter of that first word.

T

reated like a living guru, or teacher. It is taken each morning and placed on a raised platform (manji sahib) with a canopy (chanani) in the gurdwara. Worshippers bow before it when entering the room, to show their respect and honour for its place and importance.

H

omes only have a copy if they have enough space to have a special room just for the Guru Granth Sahib (often called 'Babaji's Room'). Otherwise they will have a Gutka, which contains extracts.

The Guru Granth Sahib

How do Sikhs treat people who break laws?

> 'There can be no worship without performing good deeds.'
>
> AG 4

> 'A place in God's court can only be attained if we do service to others in this world.'
>
> AG 26

For Sikhs there is no distinction beetween temporal (miri) and spiritual (piri) power. Therefore the Rahit Maryada (Sikh Code of Conduct) is the standard against which Sikh individuals and communities should measure themselves. It contains:

- instructions on personal devotion and congregational prayer
- rules for gurdwara worship and the reading of the Guru Granth Sahib
- a list of beliefs and prohibited practices
- details about naming, marriage and death services
- guidance on seva (service), langar (shared meal), and amrit pahul (initiation ceremony)

At the heart of Sikh belief and practice is the principle of caring – this is not an optional extra, and neither is religion about saving one's own soul. Where things do go wrong, and people do things that they should not, it is because of what Sikh's call haumai. This is ignorance and self-centredness, which result in people not seeing God in others as well as in themselves, and imagining that they are the most important thing around. Once a person realises this it enables them to be supportive and forgiving towards others who make mistakes.

Sikhs believe that for some serious crimes, capital punishment may be necessary, but that it should never be carried out in revenge.

What about capital punishment?

Capital punishment is when a person is put to death, as a punishment for a crime. Sometimes it is referred to as 'the death penalty'. In the United Kingdom it has been abolished since 1970.

There are many issues when thinking about capital punishment:

JON: Did you see that film last night, with the execution on? He got just what he deserved!

SARAH: You are so sad! It was horrible. How can anyone enjoy watching someone else be tortured and die?

JON: He wasn't being tortured. He was put in the electric chair because he had murdered someone else. He got what he deserved.

SARAH: But it's a life taken away isn't it? Surely the person that took his life away is a murderer too?

JON: They were doing a duty to other human beings. That man could have escaped prison and gone out and murdered again. With his execution it will make other people think before taking someone's life.

SARAH: So you've got proof that capital punishment is a deterrent then?

JON: What do you want? Should he be kept on Death Row for the rest of his life? Have you any idea how much it costs to keep people in prison? All that money could be spent on schools and hospitals.

SARAH: But what about those people who are wrongly accused, and mistakes happen. There's no point saying sorry after they are dead.

JON: But those are one-off's. Society needs to be protected from cold-blooded murderers.

SARAH: So you would say that two wrongs make a right!! Have you any idea what people are executed for throughout the world? Many people are executed for crimes such as prostitution, practising a religion or speaking out against a government. Look up the Amnesty website and you'll see what I'm talking about.

Look it up

http://www.amnesty.org

Task

- Look up the Amnesty website, and note down ten facts that you didn't know about capital punishment.
- Make a list of the arguments for and against capital punishment from the dialogue between Sarah and Jon.

What about religions and capital punishment?

Often there may be state issues that religions have to consider. One such issue is capital punishment. Although abolished in 1970, there have been various attempts to get Parliament to re-instate it for certain types of crimes; during these debates, religious believers have had to consider how their religious beliefs affect such an issue.

CHRISTIANITY ✞

Generally:

- Christians often have personal considerations on this issue
- Reference to the commandment 'Thou shalt not kill'
- All life is sacred
- Jesus taught compassion not revenge
- The Old Testament says 'an eye for an eye'

SOCIETY OF FRIENDS (Quakers):

- Have campaigned against capital punishment since 1818
- Reverence for all is important
- Punishments should be used to reform

JUDAISM ♉

- Today there are many Jewish views on the issue
- In the Torah, some crimes were punishable by death
- Deuteronomy 17: 6 states 'A person shall be put to death only on the testimony of two or more witnesses.
- Leviticus 24: 17–18 states 'Anyone who commits murder shall be put to death.'
- In Israel, the death sentence is only used for genocide or treason

BUDDHISM ☸

- Buddhists argue about its appropriateness in deterring crimes
- The first precept deplores the taking of life
- Buddhism acknowledges that it depends on state law
- It is against the Buddhist principle of metta (loving kindness)
- It is also against the principle of karuna (compassion)

HINDUISM ॐ

- It is against the principle of ahimsa
- Used to depend on caste
- Individuals are likely to suffer for their wrongdoing in this life or the next

ISLAM ☪

- Two crimes are seen as serious enough for execution: murder and openly attacking Islam
- Surah 17:33 forbids the taking of life 'Nor take life – which Allah has made sacred, except for just cause.'

SIKHISM ☬

- Wrongdoing is likely to be punished in this life or the next
- Capital punishment is not contrary to the Sikh World View, and may need to be used

Task

Look at each of the statements below. Decide which you think the religions you are studying would agree with, and explain why.

- If someone killed my best friend I would kill them
- All human life is sacred
- The death penalty is no deterrent
- Life imprisonment is more of a deterrent
- The victim's family should decide the fate of the murderer
- Forgiveness is important
- Everyone bears the image of God
- We have the responsibility to care for the poor and the powerless

It is important to build on prior learning. Look back over your work so far, and note down the issues in other topics you have studied in this course that have links with this unit. Issues such as sanctity of life, justice and fairness, reconciliation, etc.

Exam Tip

Many candidates lose marks because they do not use technical terms correctly, and do not even give the proper name for the religious traditions they are writing about. Although marks are not taken off for these inaccuracies, it is not possible to gain full marks if they are incorrect.

Task

- Look at the examples of errors below. Can you give the correct terms for each?

Naming religious traditions:
'Katholicks'
'Prodestants'
'Hinduists'
'Buddhas'
'Sihks'
'Islams'
'Jewadists'

Technical terms:	
'reconsilation'	'foregive'
'uthenasha'	'fetus'
'kishatrias'	'scared'
'tempel'	'mosck'
'sinagoge'	'koran'
'pasifist'	'religios'
'sancity'	'inosense'

When Secular and Religious meet

The term 'secular' is used to refer to things that are not specifically religious. So, the Government of most countries is a secular government; and many of the laws of the land are secular laws – they are devised by the secular government and enforced by the police and the secular courts.

In some countries there is a partnership between the church or main religious group and the state authorities.

In Britain, for example, the Church of England is the 'established church', and as such has a right to speak and vote in matters of government, and the Queen is actually the Head of the Church. People also have a right to the ceremonies.

Religious wedding ceremonies are recognised by the state as legal

A Bishop in the House of Lords

Many people choose to mark the passing of a loved-one with a religious ceremony

The Queen is the head of the Church of England as well as figure head of the State

Some countries are called 'Islamic States', as they exercise the Shariah Laws – here the religious laws are the laws of state, and apply to everyone, regardless of their religion. Shariah means 'straight path' and gives both rules and punishments. It is based on the Qur'an and Sunnah, and is believed to be relevant for all time.

In Judaism, there are special rabbinic courts, called Beth Din, which decide on matters to do with the religious way of life, including ceremonies. This includes deciding which products are allowed to be called kosher. Beth Din ('house of justice') does not have a jury, but the judges themselves question the witnesses and give their verdict. They do not try criminal cases, but cases connected with particular Jewish issues, e.g. conversions to Judaism, supervising the production of kosher foods, and the granting of Jewish divorce bills (gets).

Within Judaism there is the concept of duty and loyalty to the state, and in synagogue services in Britain, for example, prayers will be said for the royal family and the government.

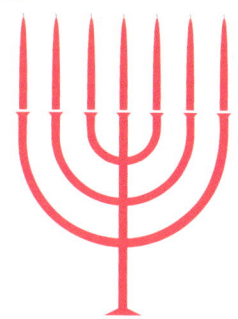

This logo, which, appears on food packets, means the food has been certified as kosher

In Sikhism, the Rahit Maryada, or Code of Conduct, is a religious law all Sikhs should follow. It also lays down the requirements for managing and conducting religious rituals and ceremonies in the gurdwaras, so it is observed by gurdwara management committees.

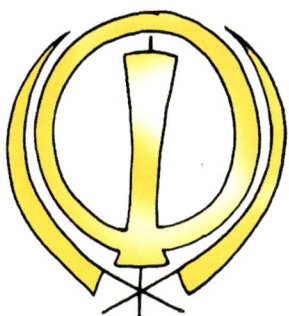

Members of the management committee of a gurdwara

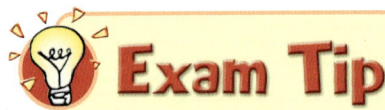

Exam Tip

When giving an answer about a religion's teachings or practices, be sure you give specific examples. Too many candidates do not describe the content clearly, or in sufficient detail.

Q *'Render to Caesar the things that are Caesar's and to God the things that are God's.' Mark 12: 17*

What do Christians believe Jesus meant when he said these words? [4]

Look at the two answers below. Neither of them has given a full answer. Can you explain why? Choose one answer, and amend it so that it would gain full marks.

Answer A	Answer B
I think Christians believe this passage tells them that they should obey the government of the day, even if that means paying your taxes, and not trying to avoid them. Jesus was saying that people should respect the government as they are the legitimate rulers.	Christians believe Jesus was saying that they have responsibility to pay their taxes and be good citizens; but they also have a duty to give God their praise and worship. Doing one should not be an excuse for not doing the other. A true Christian will respect and try to obey God and the proper authorities.

What if the law is wrong?

There have been times in history when the secular laws have been wrong. Look at the following images and decide what it was that is now thought wrong, and why.

Sometimes, it appears that there may be a clash between sacred and secular laws. Jesus was presented with a dilemma of this sort, by the Pharisees:

'And they came and said to him, "Teacher, we know that you are true, and care for no man; for you do not regard the position of men, but truly teach the way of God. Is it lawful to pay taxes to Caesar, or not? Should we pay them, or should we not?" But knowing their hypocrisy, he said to them, "Why put me to the test? Bring me a coin, and let me look at it." And they brought one. And he said to them, "Whose likeness and inscription is this?" They said to him, "Caesar's". Jesus said to them, "Render to Caesar the things that are Caesar's, and to God the things that are God's." And they were amazed at him.'

Mark 12: 13–17

The question put to Jesus was really a trap, for if he had said people should not pay their taxes to Caesar, then the Pharisees would have been able to criticise Jesus for inciting rebellion against their Roman rulers. If Jesus had merely said people should pay Caesar, then they would have been able to criticise him for not bringing God into it at all.

Christians see in this passage a clear reference to Jesus commending his followers to be good citizens; he tells them that if it is a requirement to pay taxes, then they should be paid. But he also makes it clear that when such secular rules do affect us, we should not use that as an excuse for not giving to God what he is due as well.

At other times it is not so clear, and when sacred and secular laws conflict, the individual has to think through their conscience, and make a decision. In this circumstance it may be that a person's conscience will tell them what they ought to do.

A Christian traffic warden has infuriated his Miami employer by refusing to write traffic tickets as a matter of principle. William Oertwig Jr, 47, hasn't written a ticket in two years and argues that police powers shouldn't be used to collect cash. He has been demoted and is suing Miami-Dade County, claiming the training manual says tickets are given at the officer's discretion. He said, 'I believe that by educating and informing the motorist, I am accomplishing traffic enforcement.'

Evening Standard, Friday 7th July 2000

Check it out

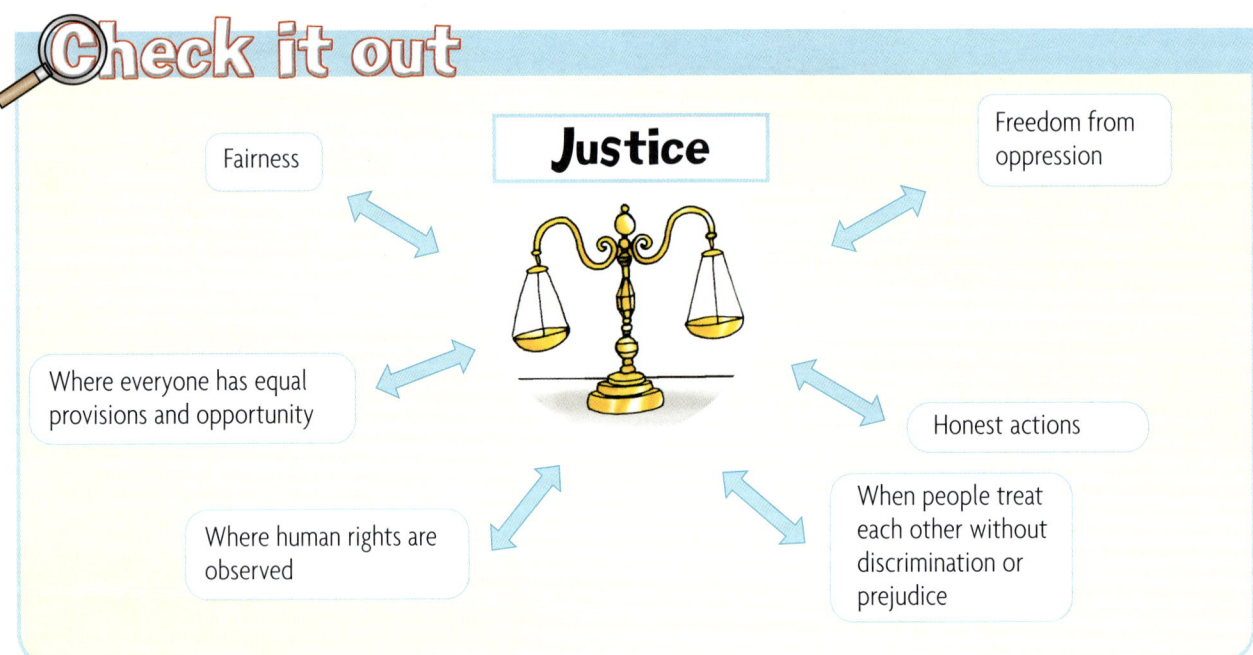

Fairness

Justice

Freedom from oppression

Where everyone has equal provisions and opportunity

Honest actions

Where human rights are observed

When people treat each other without discrimination or prejudice

Check it out

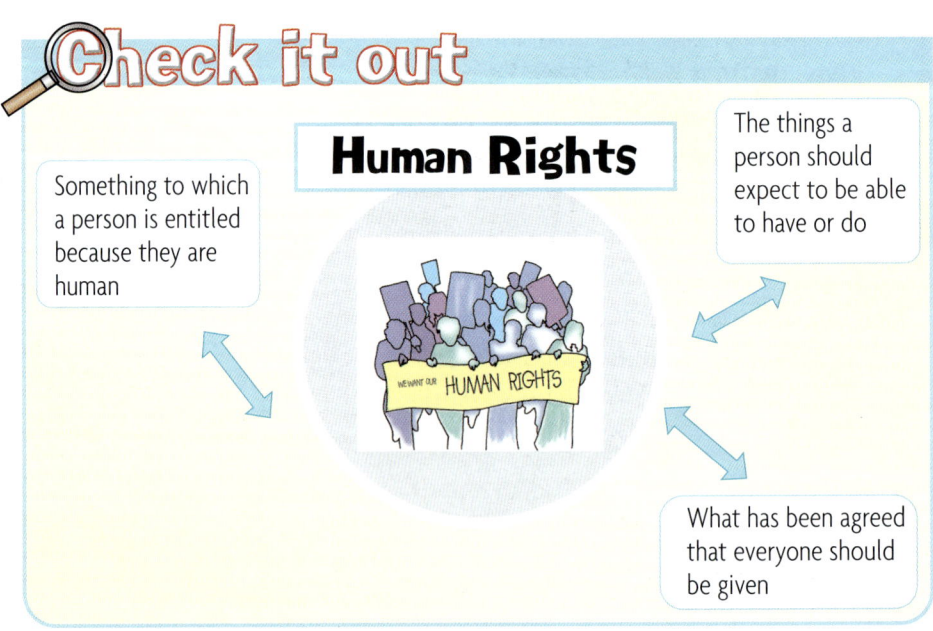

Something to which a person is entitled because they are human

Human Rights

The things a person should expect to be able to have or do

WE WANT OUR HUMAN RIGHTS

What has been agreed that everyone should be given

Often, religious leaders have been in the front line of campaigning for those who do not have the basic human rights, or who face serious discrimination and prejudice. Study the following examples, and consider carefully how their religious convictions led them to do what they did.

CHRISTIANITY ✝	*OSCAR ROMERO*

1. Oscar Romero was born in El Salvador in 1917. After training to be a carpenter he decided to become a priest and was ordained in 1942. He became Archbishop of El Salvador in 1977.	2. In the 1960's there was much crime and corruption in El Salvador. Some people were very wealthy, but many people were very poor. To begin with, Romero decided not to speak out against all the corruption that he saw.

3. His views changed after a close friend of his was murdered. He knew that he had to speak out against the injustices, and openly criticised the government. He held meetings which had been banned by the government.	4. Protestors in the church became targets of violence. Government slogans included 'Be a patriot – kill a priest.' After many threats, on 24 March 1980, soldiers burst into the cathedral and gunned Romero down while he was celebrating the Mass.

Look it up

www.Westminsterabbey.org/tour/martyrs

BUDDHISM ☀	DALAI LAMA
1. The Dalai Lama was born in Tibet in 1935. When China invaded Tibet many Buddhists were beaten and killed.	2. The Dalai Lama escaped to India, where he lives today.
3. While he has been in exile he has worked for Tibet to be free from Chinese rule and for peace.	4. In 1989 he was given the Nobel Peace Prize.

Look it up

http://www.buddhanet.net

HINDUISM ॐ

MAHATMA GANDHI

1. Mahatma Gandhi was born in India in 1869, and after studying law in London he returned to India which was governed by British rulers.

2. Gandhi began work in 1894 to use peaceful means to let Indians govern themselves.

3. He used many forms of civil disobedience, including hunger strike, burning of identity passes, and leading a march against the Salt Tax.

4. For all his actions Gandhi always used non-violence as he believed that all life was sacred. He was assassinated in 1948, but even as he lay dying he forgave his killer.

Look it up

www.gandhi.org

ISLAM ☪

PROPHET MOHAMMAD

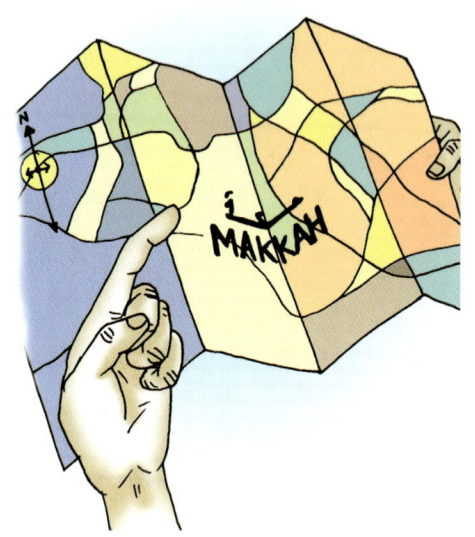

1. When the Prophet Muhammad was born about 570 CE there were many corrupt practices happening in Makkah.

2. As a young man he showed his concern for justice by becoming a member of a group to protect the safety and rights of strangers. He was called Al-Amin 'The Trustworthy'.

3. After the revelation of the Qur'an to The Prophet, there are many examples of times when he spoke out and acted against the corrupt practices of his day. He showed great respect for women, disagreed with female infanticide, and rid the Kaabah of the idols which had been placed there.

4. For many Muslims they will try to follow the examples set by The Prophet through his actions (sunnah) and sayings (hadith).

Look it up
www.islam4kids.com

JUDAISM	JUDAS MACCABEUS

1. Antiochus IV was a Syrian-Greek king who captured many countries. He then forced people to worship Greek gods. Antiochus sent out an army which broke into the Temple in Jerusalem and destroyed any signs of the religion they saw. Jews who resisted him were killed.	2. Judah led a revolt against the armies. He used many heroic actions to lead a small army in revolt. In keeping with Jewish law he sent home those who were afraid, newly-weds or planting fields.

3. In 168 BCE Judah led the Maccabeans to the enemy's camp. Although they were far greater in number than the Maccabees, Judah's strategy was successful, and drove the armies out.	4. Judah went to re-dedicate the Temple, and it was then that the miracle happened – lights continually burning for eight days (now celebrated at the festival of Hanukkah).

 **Look it up**

www.virtualchanukah.com

SIKHISM ☬	GURU GOBIND SINGH

1. After the time of Guru Nanak, there had been persecution of many Sikhs and their Gurus. Guru Gobind Singh (1666–1708 CE) was the last of the ten living Gurus.	2. He formed a Khalsa (community of the pure) of Sikhs who would be prepared to die for their faith and what they thought was true.

3. The Khalsa fought many battles to defend the Sikh community.	4. Today anyone who agrees to accept the rules governing the Sikh community can receive amrit, and enter the Khalsa.

 **Look it up**

http://www.sikhs.org/guru1.htm

Exam Tip

Sometimes you will be asked for the name and a brief description of the work of an individual or agency.

Always mention specific things done by the person or agency – be brief and concise *and make the comments relevant to the unit*. Always read the question carefully, so that you are clear about the focus for the answer. DO NOT just write all you know about the person or agency!

Task

- Using the IMPACT formula (see page 118) construct an outline for two of the individuals above in the religious traditions you are studying.

- You may also like to find out about other individuals or organisations that do a similar kind of work in those religious traditions.

TEST IT OUT

(a) State **two** human rights   [2]

(b) What is conscience?   [2]

(c) 'Render to Caesar the things that are Caesar's, and to God the things that are God's.' [Mark 12: 17]

   What do Christians believe Jesus meant when he said these words?   [4]

(d) Explain why some believers would consider it important to protect the weak.   [4]

(e) Describe the attitude to capital punishment from **two** different religious traditions.   [6]

(f) 'The main aim of punishment is to protect society.'

   Do you agree? Give reasons or evidence for your answer, showing that you have thought about more than one point of view.   [6]

5 Suffering and Evil

The Big Picture

In what ways do people suffer?

Why do people suffer?

How do people cope with suffering?

What is evil?

Why is there evil?

Questions to ask

Words to know, understand and use: ▼

GOOD

EVIL

SUFFERING

INNOCENCE

FREEWILL

FATE

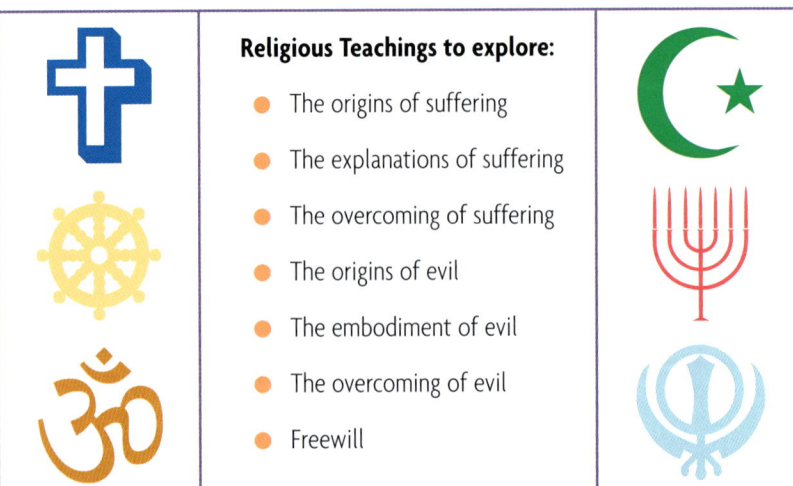

Religious Teachings to explore:

- The origins of suffering
- The explanations of suffering
- The overcoming of suffering
- The origins of evil
- The embodiment of evil
- The overcoming of evil
- Freewill

Check it out

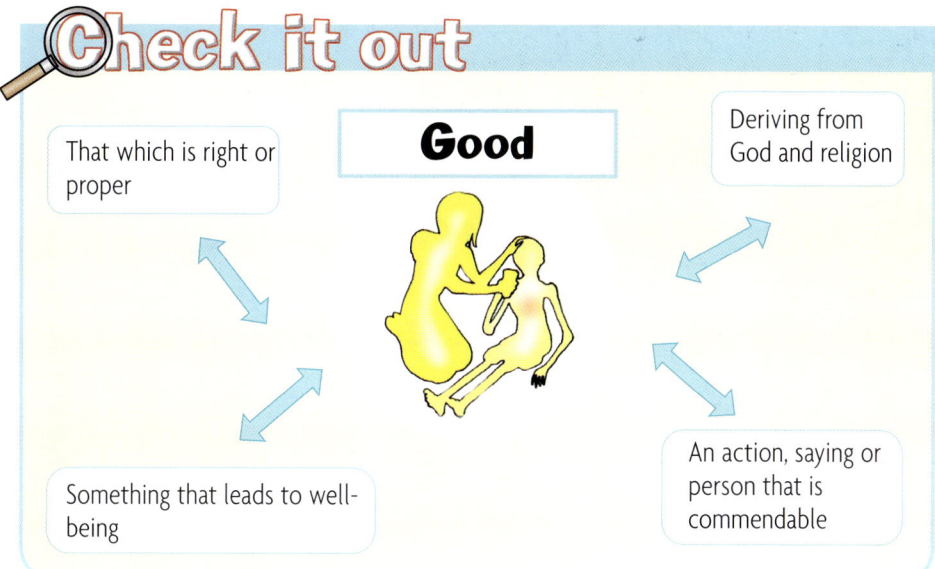

That which is right or proper

Good

Deriving from God and religion

Something that leads to well-being

An action, saying or person that is commendable

I THINK "GOOD AND EVIL" ARE VERY HARD TO DEFINE...

1-20

I HAVE MY OWN OPINION, OF COURSE, SUCH AS IT IS...

© 1981 United Feature Syndicate, Inc.

FOR INSTANCE, WHEN I'M WALKING DOWN THE STREET, I ALWAYS TRY TO AVOID STEPPING ON A BUG...

SCHULZ

HURRAY! HURRAY! CLAP CLAP CLAP CLAP CLAP!

Task

There are many opportunities for 'out of school learning' experiences during your studies. This is a living issues course, so it is important to discuss the issues with friends, family and other people, and to listen to and analyse their responses.

Interview six people and ask them to define good and evil. Once you have all their responses in front of you, you might want to consider the following

- What areas are similar?

- Which did people find the hardest to explain?

- How influential were religious teachings and ideas?

How do people suffer?

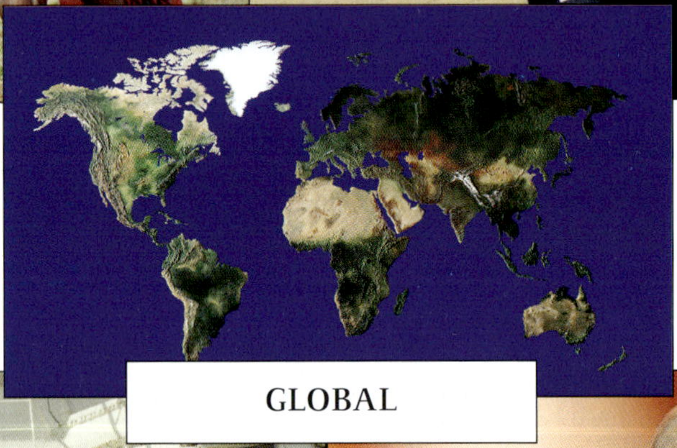

GLOBAL

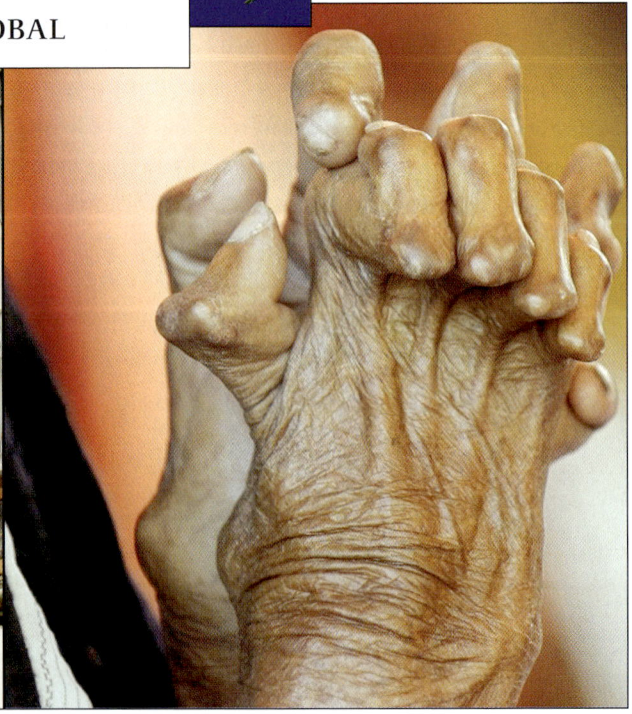

PERSONAL

Why do people suffer?

When people suffer they often wonder, 'why?'

> Why me, and not someone else?

> Why has this happened at all?

> What have we done to deserve this?

For as many different types of suffering there are as many different reasons.

Why people suffer is a question known as an 'ultimate question'. That means a question that asks about things that are really concerning fundamental principles in life itself. They are the hardest questions that can be asked, because it is difficult – some would say impossible – to get a completely final and conclusive answer to them. No matter how clever someone is or how long they have lived, there is no *one* certain and categorical answer.

When people consider the causes of suffering, there are many different beliefs. For some people, suffering is connected with good and evil, and the balance between these in their own lives, and in the world as a whole. This means that they see some of the suffering as being from their own decisions and actions, but also that some of it is beyond themselves and their own actions and thinking.

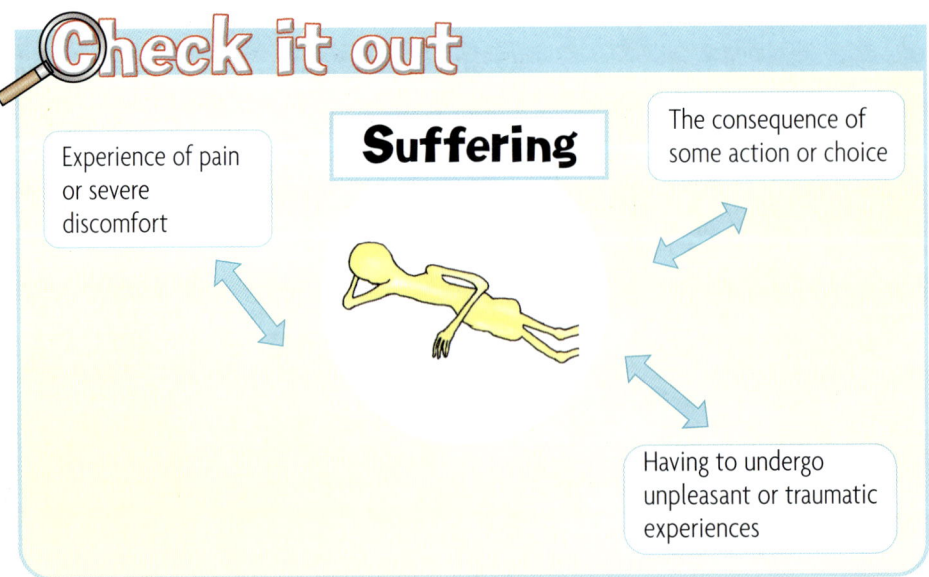

Check it out

Experience of pain or severe discomfort

Suffering

The consequence of some action or choice

Having to undergo unpleasant or traumatic experiences

Check it out

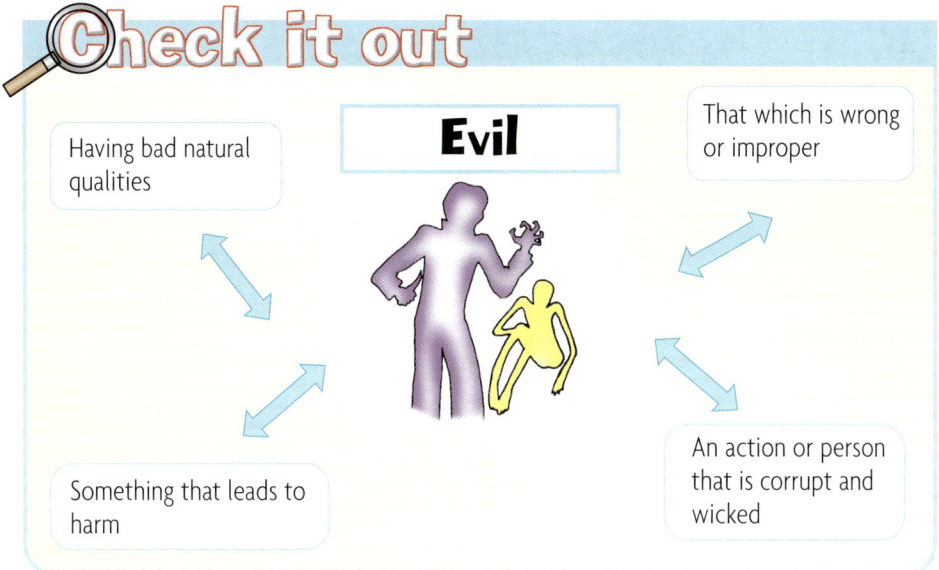

Having bad natural qualities

Evil

That which is wrong or improper

Something that leads to harm

An action or person that is corrupt and wicked

The question of evil is an example of 'an ultimate question'. That means that it is a question to which there may be different answers and none of them are wrong. Each person will have the answer that they consider is right. This might have been formed by their own experiences; influenced by family and friends; religious teachings and their own reasonings.

Many examples of ultimate questions can be seen on the wall below:

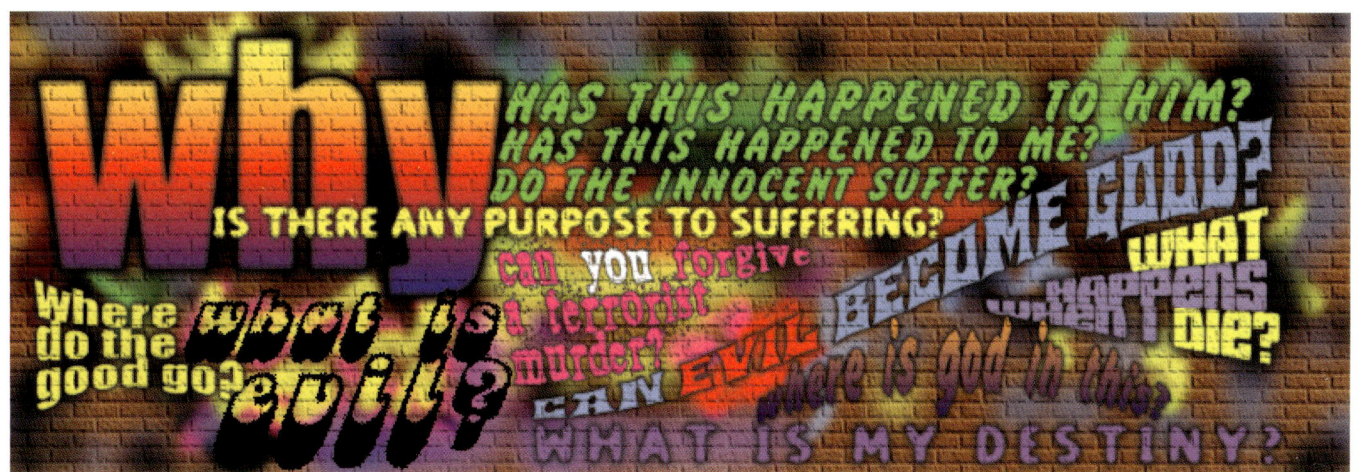

Task

- Can you think of any more questions?

Choose any two, and write an answer to each for a problem page.

What about religions and suffering and evil?

All religions have some form of answers as to why there is suffering. Many religions make a connection with fate and freewill.

Check it out

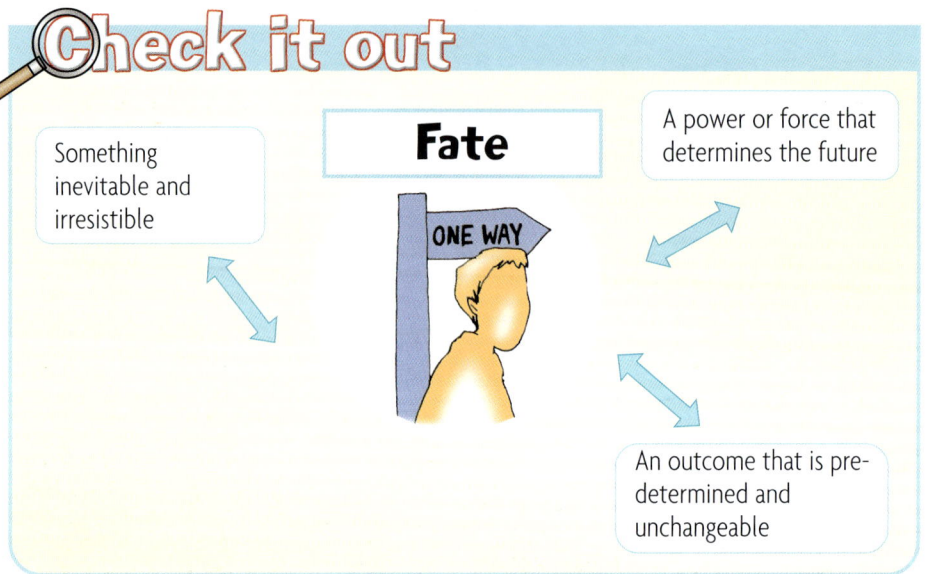

Something inevitable and irresistible

Fate

A power or force that determines the future

ONE WAY

An outcome that is pre-determined and unchangeable

Check it out

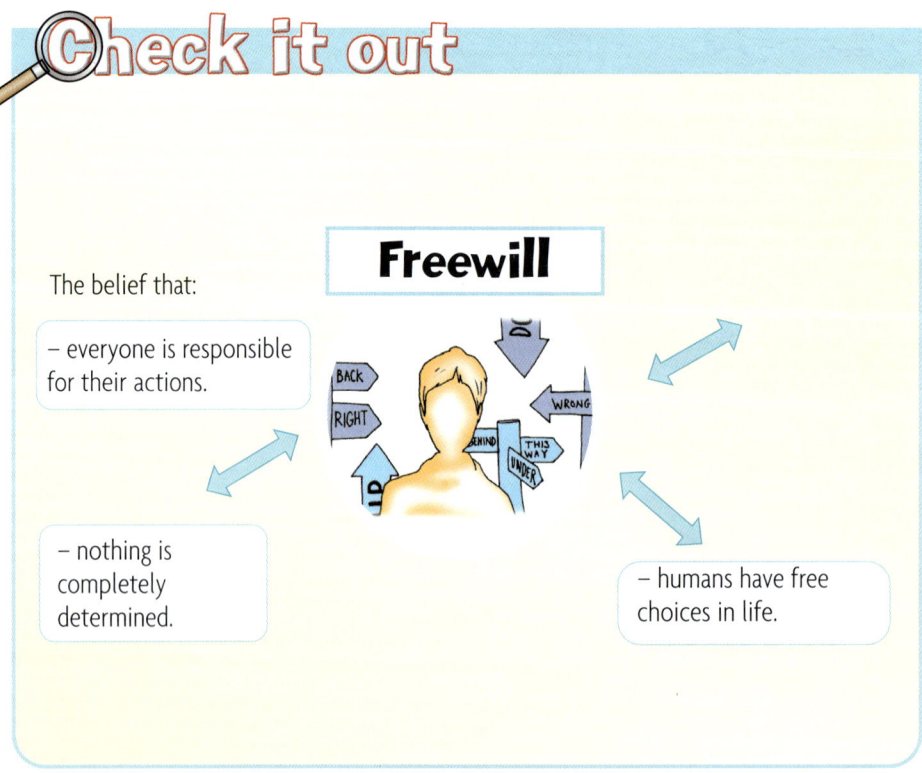

The belief that:

– everyone is responsible for their actions.

Freewill

BACK
RIGHT

WRONG
THIS WAY
UNDER

– nothing is completely determined.

– humans have free choices in life.

Check it out

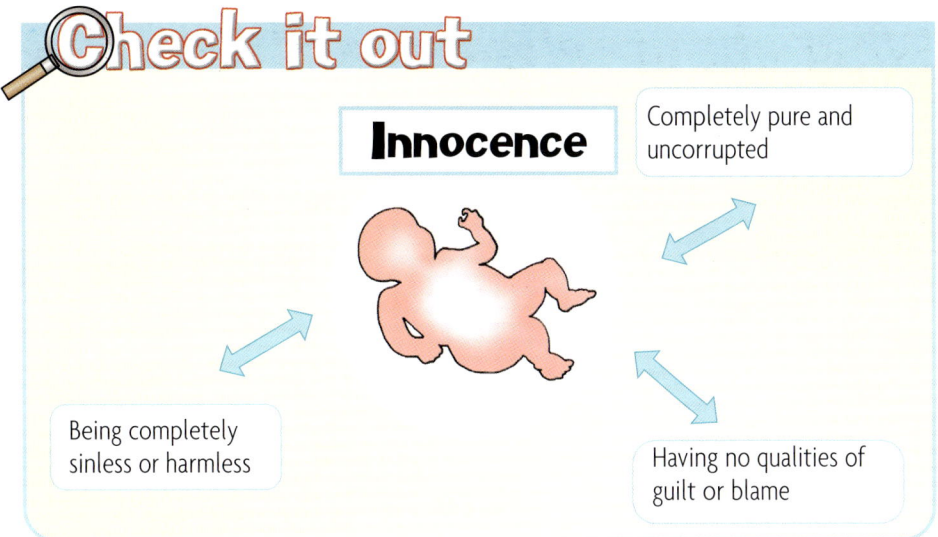

Innocence

Completely pure and uncorrupted

Being completely sinless or harmless

Having no qualities of guilt or blame

Every day newspapers and television show us how many people suffer through no fault of their own. Many believers consider that innocent suffering can have a divine purpose and that it is impossible for all life to have no experiences of suffering.

'God, having placed good and evil in our power, has given us full freedom of choice; he does not keep back the unwilling, but embraces the willing.'

John Chrysostom

For Christians, freewill is something God gave to human beings. This means they have the ability to choose to do good and the ability to choose to do evil. As a result of 'original sin', people tend to find it easier to choose to do evil or wrong, but with God's help can learn to choose good. There is also the way of confession and forgiveness to amend for past failures. Fate is not a Christian idea.

'An evil deed committed does not immediately bear fruit, just as milk does not curdle at once: but like a smouldering fire covered with ashes, it remains with the fool until the moment it ignites and burns him.'

Dhammapada 69, 73

For Buddhists, the connection between fate and freewill are explained by the law of karma. This is a form of justice by which actions control the future. So our present fate is a result of our past actions.

FATE

FREEWILL

'In proportion to the extent of one's religious or irreligious actions in this life, one must enjoy or suffer the corresponding reactions of his karma in the next.'

Bhagavat Purana 6.1.45

For Hindus, the connection beetween fate and freewill is explained by the law of karma. This is a form of justice by which past actions control the future. So present fate is a result of our past actions.

 For Muslims, the idea of iktisab is important, this means that although each individual action is foreordained, the person must still 'acquire' or 'merit' responsibility for it by identifying himself with it. So there is no fate in Islam, in the sense of helpless abandonment; rather there is the idea of co-operating with Allah, studying His will and bringing oneself into unity with His will.

'Whatever of good befalleth thee (O man) it is from Allah, and whatever of ill befalleth thee it is from thyself.'

Surah iv. 79

 Many Jews believe that what happens in life is decreed by God. In the Talmud there is a descriptiion of an unborn child being shown the fate that awaits it. However, there is an emphasis that the one thing every person can do is learn the law and therefore, whether the person is good or bad remains in the person's freewill. Certain things are considered by genes, but you have the choice to set up your personality and choose to be good (yetzer ha-tov) or bad (yetzer ha-ray).

 'Man has been given freewill; if he wishes to turn toward the good ways and to be righteous, the power is in his own hands; if he wishes to run towards the evil way and to be wicked, the power is likewise in his own hands.'

Moses Maimonodies

 FATE

 FREEWILL

 For Sikhs, ultimately everything that happens is within the will of God (hukam). It is important that people should live in obedience to God's will, by choosing to meditate on God's name, and setting one's heart and mind on God and on selfless service to others (sewa). Choosing to perform the right actions determines liberation, and union with God; attachment to the world (maya) leads to greater self-centredness (man-mukh). This tendency to do so is called haumai – but it can be overcome.

 'You are blessed by being born human, it is an opportunity which has been given to you to meet your God.'

Adi Granth 378

'O my soul, you have emanated from the light of God, know your true essence.'

Adi Granth 441

'Christians believe that everyone has freewill to perform which actions they choose.'

Why do you think this response does not answer the question? What points are made in the quote that have not been referred to in the answer?

 The Lord gave, and the Lord has taken away; blessed be the name of the Lord.' [Job 1:21]

What do Christians believe this passage teaches about suffering?

 Exam Tip

When a question quotes a specified text, think carefully about the meaning of the text. If you refer to a text in your answer, check that it is really about the question being asked, and make sure you comment on the quote. If you just quote a text, without adding anything, you will not be given any marks.

CHRISTIANITY ✠ on suffering and evil

For Christians, suffering is seen to have entered the world through the God-given ability of freewill. Many would see the story of the creation in Genesis as stating clearly that humans were created with the ability to know and worship God, and to look after the world as his stewards. However, there was a free choice to accept or reject following God's ways. The story of 'the fall' is seen to illustrate the choice to be selfish or self-centred (and so do wrong or sin), rather than to choose the path of willing obedience (and so do right, or good). The idea that humanity finds it easier to choose the selfish way, is caused by what is known as 'original sin'. Christians believe that this indicates that human nature is not perfect, but that through faith and discipline, it can overcome the tendency to sin.

As a result, this freewill can also lead to suffering, in the sense that there is 'moral' evil in the world – where people choose to do things that will lead to pain or suffering, for themselves or others. Evangelical Christians, and those in denominations such as Pentecostal and Apostolic, would say in addition, that as a result of human sin, the perfect world God created has become contaminated, and so there will also be 'natural' evil – where the natural events of the earth and its elements, sometimes lead to suffering or disaster. Others might say that it is also finite – that is, having limits; so there are bound to be accidents, death and decay.

But most Christians also believe that God is neither ignorant nor un-feeling about the suffering of humanity. Indeed, they would say that he is compassionate and understanding, and does bring good out of suffering. Christians see that, with faith and trust in God, suffering can help to develop people's character, their inner strength and their ability to overcome suffering, and succeed in the face of it.

The story of Job is a classic example to which Christians refer. You can read about this in the section on Judaism (see page 115).

Many Christians would also refer to the example of Jesus, who being God in the flesh, still chose to endure suffering and pain, in order to achieve a greater good.

Christian teaching is that Jesus was the perfect man because he was also God, and as such did not deserve to be put to death on the cross. However, his death and resurrection were to bring an end to death and suffering forever, because Jesus took the punishment for sin, and opened a way to God and his forgiveness. His resurrection offers a certain hope, and the promise of a new heaven and earth.

In the same way, Christians would also see that suffering is a way of participating in the saving work of Jesus, and the Roman Catholic catechism states this point.

Christ of St. John of the Cross painted in 1951 by Salvadov Dali

Evil

Many Christians believe that there is a power or force for evil in the world, that 'opposes' the power of God. To many Christians, evil is personified in the form of Satan, or the Devil. He is said to have once been an angel, who turned against God, and was banished from heaven. His exploits in tempting humans and trying to stop goodness and peace are limited; Christ's resurrection and living power through the Holy Spirit offer a chance for humans to overcome them, and at the Last Day he will be completely defeated.

Some Christians would also point to the fact that the world is not perfect, and so there is inevitably going to be wrong and evil. In this way, the physical 'evil' that happens in the world is not malevolent – just a natural happening.

As regards evil caused by human decision, most Christians are united in saying that this is not God's fault. They would also say that God offers humanity the opportunity to work together, and in partnership with God, to work for and achieve a better, more caring and less selfish world.

Heaven and Hell

Christian denominations are united in their understanding and beliefs about certain aspects of life after death and judgement, and all generally teach that:

- When a person dies their souls do not cease to exist

- The soul moves on to another life – in heaven or hell

- There is a judgement which determines where the soul goes

- The destination is determined by two things:

  ■ A person's response to Jesus and his teachings

  ■ The way a person responds to those in need on earth

- God determines the time for a person to die

- After death, the body is committed to the ground or is cremated

- There is a resurrection of the body – to new life: not immortality, but resurrected life

- This resurrection, for the believer, is a sharing in the victory over death won by Jesus

- While death is a tragedy, a Christian burial service reminds all that death is not the end

Roman Catholics would also refer to purgatory – a place of preparation for heaven. Only the very good go straight to heaven; so there is a responsibility to pray for the dead (requiem mass).

Most Protestant denominations would rarely pray for the dead. They would stress the importance of personal faith and repentance.

Orthodox burial services stress the hope of resurrection.

Within some denominations there are particular differences or emphases. For example, some Christians do not believe that there will be a hell, because they see God as all loving, so everyone will be forgiven.

BUDDHISM ✹ on suffering and evil

The truth of suffering is the basic truth of Buddhism. It was an essential part of Siddhartha's enlightenment that he recognised the role of Maya-illusion. The Four Noble Truths show that:

- All is dukkha (suffering)

- The cause of suffering is craving/greed and desire

- This can be stopped

- The way to stop it is to follow the Eightfold Path

Many of the Buddha's actions were to help others understand about dukkha. An example of this can be found in the story of Kisagotami. When Kisa finds her baby has died she goes to the Buddha to find help.

K: Please help me and bring my baby back to life

B: Fetch a mustard seed from a house where no one has suffered

K: Now I understand; everyone faces suffering in their life

Evil

As Buddhism is not dualistic it does not divide good from evil. It recognizes evil as a limitation and so relative. All evil is traced to desire for self. The basic evil is the idea of separateness and the Buddhist goal is the removal of evil by the eradication of all sense of separate selfhood.

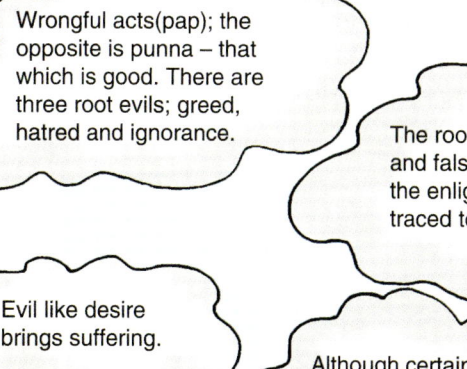

Wrongful acts(pap); the opposite is punna – that which is good. There are three root evils; greed, hatred and ignorance.

The root of all evil is ignorance and false views – these obscure the enlightened mind. So evil is traced to oneself.

Evil like desire brings suffering.

Although certain acts in the Dhammapada are termed as evil (such as killing, lying), greed is seen at the root.

HINDUISM ॐ on suffering and evil

Hindus consider goodness and evil as parts of life coming from God. This is why the god Kali is believed to be good as well as evil as by causing suffering she encourages people to be detached as she constantly destroys the earthly pleasures that people enjoy so much.

Sometimes suffering is considered as part of one of the god's actions and so Hindus try to keep the deities happy. Shiva is considered the lord of destruction and carries a thunderbolt while driving his chariot. He is often portrayed as Nataraja stamping out the devil and wearing a serpent around his neck, and wearing a garland of skulls. Hindus often blame Shiva for natural disasters such as earthquakes, floods and hurricanes.

Hindus believe that to escape suffering, it is important not to become attached to worldly goods which can be an illusion or maya. The Puranas suggests that suffering is a result of people's sinful actions (papa) in previous reincarnations – this is the law of karma.

Most Hindus want to achieve Moksha, which is the final release or liberation and will free them from any further suffering.

Shiva

ISLAM ☪ on suffering and evil

For Muslims, everything that happens is part of the will and plan (qadr) of Allah. This means that suffering and hardship are part of Allah's great plan, even though people may not be able to see or understand that. The fact is, in Islam, Allah's knowledge is greater than humans, and humans will never be able to comprehend Allah's will and purpose.

Basic to Islamic teaching is the idea that life itself is a test. Humans are given life, the created world and other people for which to care. The purpose of Islam is to enable people to achieve this responsibility. In this way, suffering itself is a kind of test; a proving of one's faith; a showing of one's resistance to the tempting of Satan (Shaytan; or Iblis).

Shaytan being defeated

Good can, however result from suffering and evil, because it is a greater good when people resist temptation, and follow in the way of the Prophet Muhammad. Muslims believe he is the model example for humans to follow.

But Allah is also known as Ar-Rahman (The Merciful), Ar-Rahim (The Compassionate), and Al-Karim (The Generous), and so those who resist Shaytan, and follow the way laid down, will be rewarded in the afterlife.

Evil

Many Muslims believe evil comes from Shaytan. The Qur'an tells (Surah 7, 11–13) how he refused Allah's command to bow down before Adam, as he felt he was nobler than a human being made out of clay. As a result of such pride and disobedience, Allah banished him from heaven, and now he tempts people to turn from Allah and do wrong.

The Qur'an warns people to resist such temptation, and reminds them that all evil acts are noted by two angels, who will have the record of a person's life on the final judgement.

At death, those who know that Allah is the one true God, and that Muhammad is his Prophet, will remain in comfort until the Day of Resurrection; all others will be in torment. On the Judgement Day (Qayamah), everyone will be resurrected, and will be judged by Allah according to their actions and their faith. Believers, who have tried to follow the way of Islam, will have their sins forgiven, and will go to heaven – a beautiful garden, full of pleasures. Disbelievers, who have turned their back on Allah and his ways, will be sent to hell – a blazing fire that never ends.

JUDAISM on suffering and evil

In one sense, suffering results from the presence of freewill. The description in Genesis explains that God gave humanity freewill, and in so doing, gave them the potential for choosing to do either good or evil. In another sense, suffering comes from God too, as he can use it as a way of discipline, as a form of punishment for wrongdoing, as a kind of test, or a way of returning to God.

Satan Smiting Job by William Blake

The story of Job shows that someone who is a holy and good-living person can go from great success to loss and tragedy for no reason. Job's friends consider that his suffering was a result of past sins. When Job questions God, he does not give direct answers, but challenges him as to how he can question what he does. Job has to accept that God has control, even though he may not, at that time, be able to understand why this suffering is happening to him. Jews consider God to be just, merciful and holy – so it is wrong to question him.

As the story of Job states (28: 28):

> 'The fear of the Lord, that is wisdom; And to depart from evil is understanding.'

Throughout history many Jews have been persecuted for their beliefs.

Although Jewish scriptures often portray Satan as an adversary, in the Apocrypha, Satan is portrayed as representing the forces of evil. Yetzar Ha Ra is the selfish desire to do bad things, but is not considered evil in itself.

Most Jews believe that death is not the end, but the soul continues. It is believed that God is the judge, and evil will be punished. During the ten days leading up to Yom Kippur, Jews have the chance to reflect on their misdeeds and to seek atonement.

Throughout history Jews have waited and hoped for the coming of the Mashiach (Messiah) but the Messianic Age has not yet dawned.

SIKHISM on suffering and evil

Many Sikhs consider suffering as the result of human actions (haumai), and are not to be blamed on God, even though everything which happens is within his will. Because humans have the ability to know right from wrong, and so choose between them, it is open to them to follow after God's heart and learn to serve others. The Adi Granth recommends that we should give up goods which cannot accompany us after death and concentrate instead on seeking spiritual wealth and inner qualities. In seeking these, the cycle of existence can be broken, and lead to liberation (mukti).

There are, however obstacles to achieving mukti:

- Maya: sometimes called illusion, which results in a focusing on worldly things

- Manmukh: or self-centredness, as opposed to God-centredness

- The five evils:
    - Kam – lust
    - Lobh – covetousness, or greed
    - Moh – attachment to worldly things and pleasures
    - Krodh – anger
    - Ahankar – pride or arrogance

In the Adi Granth, Guru Nanak reflects to himself that it is futile to ask for pleasure when suffering comes, for both are robes that must be worn. But it is possible – and Sikhs should strive for it – to rise above suffering and gain release through obedience and trust in God.

He is the One God, who is eternal truth, creator, who is timeless, immanent, self-existent and beyond the cycle of birth and death.

Sikhs see the soul as a minute spark of the Eternal Soul, and so it will never die. Death is not the end, but the beginning of another phase. So, a combination of good works and religious acts of devotion help one's rebirth.

Coping with Suffering

'I am grateful for the experiences. I really feel like a man because of some of the things I had to do. I've arranged and paid for several funerals now. But it taught me what's important about living and gave me a sense of how brief our time on Earth is. It makes me think, that when I'm lying on my death bed, I want to look back and think I did something worthwhile and good. Particularly when my mother died. I spent a lot of time with her. It's devastating. You see how they're summing their life up – what they're happy about, the things they wish were different.'

Mark Everett, lead singer from *The Eels*

'A few years ago, I lost my sister in a terrible road accident; I thought I'd never be able to get over it. I will always miss her, but I've come to terms with her death now. It's made me stronger — I feel more able to deal with life's smaller problems. Nothing's as important as losing a loved one.'

Exam Tip

Use the stimulus provided in the examination paper to help you. **Never** just copy words, phrases, or simply describe the picture. The stimulus should help you remember things you have studied or discussed. It will give you ideas to write about and either explain or state your own ideas and views.

 *Explain the teaching from **one** religious tradition about overcoming suffering. [6]*

Look at the two answers on the next page. Which one do you think is the better answer and why. Now write an answer for the other religious tradition that you are studying.

Answer A	Answer B
Jesus told the parable of the Good Samaritan, where a non-Jewish man helps a Jew who has been attacked. This shows that Christians believe that they should always try and help those who suffer, and do something to end their suffering. It is a duty to God.	Jesus taught that his followers should overcome suffering with goodness. This meant 'turning the other cheek' in the face of hostility or unkindness. He told many stories to illustrate this idea, such as the Good Samaritan, and the Sheep and the Goats. By continually doing good in the face of evil and wrongdoing, Christians believe it will be overcome. To do this requires God's help through the Holy Spirit.

> For all religions it is believed that it is important to try and help those suffering around them. Every religious tradition has organisations which support others in a number of practical and spiritual ways.

CHRISTIANITY ✚

Salvation Army

I	dentify	**What is the Salvation Army?** Denomination of the Christian Church.
M	ention	**Which religious tradition does it belong to?** Christianity.
P	récis	**What are the main aims?** ● To lead people actively into a saving knowledge of Jesus Christ. ● To actively serve the community irrespective of race, belief, colour, age or sex. ● To fight for social justice.
A	cknowledge	**What are the main aspects of how it is used?** The Salvation Army runs a number of projects to support the homeless, poor, and those in need.
C	onsider	**How does the work demonstrate the teachings of the religion?** Its message is based on the Bible and its motivation is the love of God as revealed in Jesus Christ.
T	ell	**A specific example of a long or short term project** It has a team of outreach workers who support the homeless in the streets of towns and cities. They try to build up relationships with the homeless and to offer advice and support. They organize drop-in centres where rough sleepers can get food and warmth.

Look it up

http://www.salvationarmy.org.uk

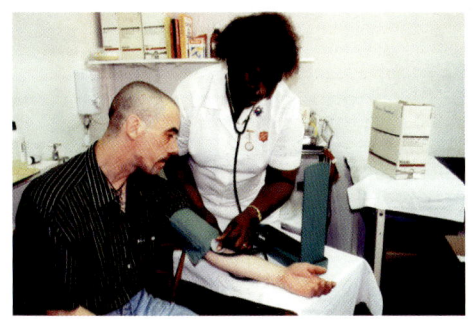

A Salvation Army nurse checking the blood pressure of a recovering alcoholic

CAFOD

I dentify	**What is CAFOD?** Catholic Fund for Overseas Development.
M ention	**Which religious tradition does it belong to?** The Roman Catholic denomination of Christianity.
P récis	**What are the main aims?** ● To educate British Roman Catholics about the need for aid. ● To raise funds to support projects with the poor.
A cknowledge	**What are the main aspects of how it is used?** It places a great importance on education and awareness raising. Activities will be organised such as 24 hour fasts, Friday Groups where people give up something; and charity shops. It has a disaster fund to deal with natural disasters and refugees in addition to long-term aid.
C onsider	**How does the work demonstrate the teachings of the religion?** By contributing to the poor and the cause of development, Roman Catholics are acting according to the Gospel tradition.
T ell	**A specific example of a long or short term project** In Brazil there are extremes of wealth and poverty. Many children live on the streets without their family and live a life of abuse and torture. CAFOD is running a scheme called 'The Community Taking Responsibility for its Children' where street children are taught to read and write and get some training to help them find work.

Look it up

http://www.cafod.org.uk

CAFOD supports schemes such as Masipag. Masipag is chemical-free farming that uses no chemical fertilisers, pesticides or herbicides

CAFOD
just one world

BUDDHISM ☸

I	dentify	**What is the Karuna Hospice Movement?** A charity which seeks to give holistic care to those with terminal illnesses.
M	ention	**Which religious tradition does it belong to?** A Buddhist based organisation.
P	récis	**What are the main aims?** To give service to people with terminal illnesses in an environment where death, dying and bereavement are openly discussed and accepted.
A	cknowledge	**What are the main aspects of their work?** To give holistic client-centred care which includes support and counselling for all the family and friends.
C	onsider	**How does the work demonstrate the teachings of the religion?** An important part of the work of the hospice is to openly discuss the impermanence of life. In the Buddha's teachings and actions he showed that all must one day die; it is a natural part of the process. This can be seen in the way that the Buddha helped the mother (Kisagotami) whose child had died. Karuna (compassion) is an important virtue in Buddhism.
T	ell	**A specific example of a long or short term project** An important aspect of the work is giving respite to the carer. This might result in hospice workers taking over duties for a short time such as acting as a caring companion, reading and writing letters, going shopping, so as to give the carer a break from time to time.

Look it up

http://www.buddhanet.net/karuna.htm

Ven. Yeshe Khadro is the Director of Karuna Hospice Services

ISLAM ☪

I	dentify	**What is Zakah?** An annual compulsory payment of money or possessions. It is one of the five pillars.
M	ention	**Which religious tradition does it belong to?** Islam.
P	récis	**What are the main aims?** By giving 2.5 per cent it 'cleanses' the rest of the Muslim's wealth and helps to develop the feeling of ummah or community.
A	cknowledge	**What are the main aspects of how it is used?** It is specifically used to help the poor, the needy, sick, imprisoned or Muslim mission workers.
C	onsider	**How does the work demonstrate the teachings of the religion?** The distribution of Zakah is determined by Allah in the Qur'an 9:60. By the rich giving to the poor the Muslim's wealth becomes pure and blessed. It also helps the giver resist greed and allows them to gain spiritual wealth.
T	ell	**A specific example of a long or short term project** Many Muslims give their Zakah to Islamic Relief who ensure that it is used for those stipulated in the Qur'an. One of the activities of Islamic Relief which Zakah may be used for is the care for welfare of orphans within many countries. The money allows them to attend school and assist in their education. It also works with orphan families to offer training and help their income.

Look it up

www.islamic-relief.com

Muslims paying
Sadaka in
Peckham, London

HINDUISM ॐ

I	dentify	**What is SEWA?** An organisation and movement established in 1972 in India for poor, self-employed women workers to try to exercise social change.
M	ention	**Which religious tradition does it belong to?** Many of its members are Hindu, but the movement has now spread to other countries such as Turkey.
P	récis	**What are the main aims?** It's principal aim is to support women to become self-reliant both economically and in decision-making. It seeks to organise women workers to obtain work security, income security, food security and social security. The struggle is against the constraints imposed by societies and economies.
A	cknowledge	**What are the main aspects of their work?** There are many aspects of the work, which include support for health-care, campaigns for mid-wives, support for vendors and home-based workers.
C	onsider	**How does the work demonstrate the teachings of the religion?** The belief in karma does not mean that there should be a lack of compassion for those who are suffering. It is important to remember that agami karma are the actions that are performed in this life which will affect the future. Gandhian thinking is the principle force of SEWA following the principles of satya (truth), ahimsa (non-violence), sarvadharma (integrating all faiths/people) and khadi (promoting local employment and reliance).
T	ell	**A specific example of a long or short term project** Thousands of women are involved in forest produce collection as their only livelihood. They care for the forest in many ways but do not receive support or technical advice. Instead, forest departments with government support often undercut the women's efforts. SEWA is supporting a project to 'feminise the forests', and involve local nursery bases. Through this way, women will obtain regular incomes.

Look it up

http://www.sewa.org

Sewa vendors

JUDAISM

I	dentify	**What is the Jewish AIDS Trust?** Jewish AIDS Trust is a charity established in 1988 to provide education, counselling and support in connection with HIV/AIDS and sexual health.
M	ention	**Which religious tradition does it belong to?** It belongs to the Jewish tradition and seeks to serve the Jewish community.
P	récis	**What are the main aims?** To provide education, counselling and support in connection with HIV/AIDS and sexual health. This includes support and counselling of those affected by HIV/AIDS, as well as awareness raising work.
A	cknowledge	**What are the main aspects of their work?** The primary focus of their work is education and awareness raising in the Jewish community. The trust also offers a completely confidential service which will seek to give support in a number of ways. Counselling is offered not only to those affected by HIV/AIDS, but also to partners, family and friends.
C	onsider	**How does the work demonstrate the teachings of the religion?** An important value in Judaism is bikkur cholim (caring for the sick), and showing chesed ve'emet (loving kindness) not only in thought but also in action. By the educational raising awareness of HIV/AIDS, the trust is exercising pikuach nefesh (saving life). Judaism also teaches that every effort should be made to relieve suffering.
T	ell	**A specific example of a long or short term project** Individual education and aware raising workshops delivered by education volunteers to the Jewish community. The Social Network and the Social Network and Practical Support System (SNAPS) also provides help in meeting the needs of people living with HIV/AIDS. This may include financial support as well as confidential counselling.

Look it up

http://www.jat-uk.org

JEWISH AIDS TRUST

JAT's primary focus is education and awareness raising

SIKHISM

I	dentify	**What is Khalsa Aid?** A Sikh organisation working throughout the world.
M	ention	**Which religious tradition does it belong to?** Sikhism
P	récis	**What are the main aims?** To provide practical relief and service to those suffering.
A	cknowledge	**What are the main aspects of their work?** Serving others in areas of social need.
C	onsider	**How does the work demonstrate the teachings of the religion?** Giving to the hungry is seen as giving to God – but only if it is genuine and from the heart. In the Guru Granth Sahib it says 'the true path to God lies in the service of our fellow beings.' The Sikh emphasis on helping others is seen in the 'langar' – a free communal eating area attached to every gurdwara. In support of the Sikh emphasis on equality Khalsa Aid tries to help all those in need irrespective of caste, creed, gender and religion. Their motto is 'recognising all human beings as one.'
T	ell	**A specific example of a long or short term project** Khalsa Aid's first mission was to Albania. They appealed to the Sangat (congregation) for food, clothing and money to help the Kosovar refugees. They have been involved in the provision of langar and aid to relieve suffering in the earthquake-torn Gujerat.

Look it up

http://www.sikhnet.com

Exam Tip

When answering a question that asks for a description of religious teachings, give clear specific points. **Never** write general 'cover-all' comments. Check carefully how many religious traditions you should write about, and write the **correct word** for the religion or religions.

Khalsa Aid provided relief for earthquake victims in Gujarat

*Explain **two** things about how Christians have tried to explain the reason for suffering and evil in the world. [4]*

Look at the answer below. Note the specific points made, as shown. Use the Levels of Response grid on page 1 to decide on a mark. Would you add anything else to the answer? If so, what?

Christians refer to the story of Adam and Eve, and the Fall in Genesis when trying to explain why there is suffering in the world. The story reminds them that the world God created was good. In his creation of human beings, he gave them freewill, so that their relationship with him, and their following of his ways would be more true and meaningful. But having freewill means that there is a choice to accept or reject. Christians believe that, through Adam and Eve, humans tend to choose to reject God's ways, and follow after selfish interests.

But this is not all negative. Christians also realise that it would not be possible to know 'goodness' if there was not also the existence of the opposite 'evil'. And, in addition, suffering and evil in the world enables people to realise human weakness or sin, and to strive to put right the wrongs done, and to overcome evil with good. There are many examples of Christians who did this, like Mother Teresa and Oscar Romero.

Reference to stories or passages from which Christians draw teachings

Use of technical terms or key concept in the answer

Including analytical comments about the teaching or belief – showing a greater level of understanding

Describing the implications of belief, and referring to examples from the religious tradition

TEST IT OUT

(a) State **two** different ways in which people suffer. [2]

(b) What is *fate?* [2]

(c) Explain why some believers think evil exists. [4]

(d) How might the example of Job help some believers in their own suffering? [4]

(e) Describe the teachings about suffering from **two** different religious traditions. [6]

(f) 'What I do with my life is my business.'

Do you agree? Give reasons or evidence for your answer, showing that you have thought about more than one point of view. [6]

Index

Entries marked in bold refer to key concepts from the specification